Black
Hollywood

Black Hollywood

The Negro in Motion Pictures

by Gary Null

A CITADEL PRESS BOOK
Published by Carol Publishing Group

Acknowledgements

Over a five-year period I had the pleasure of interviewing dozens of individuals who provided information for *Black Hollywood*. I especially want to thank the following: Ossie Davis, Brock Peters, Leigh Whipper, Fredi Washington, Noble Sissle, Lorenzo Tucker, Frederick O'Neal, Anita Bush, Rex Ingram, Otto Lindenmeyr, Sarah Donna, John Lee, Peter Boyle, Joe Franklin, Miles Kreuger, Hector Elizondo, James Rice, William Webb, Leslie Lee, Peter Noble, and Elaine Kahn. In addition, many sources supplied the hundreds of photographs, including Lorenzo Tucker, Joe Franklin, Warner Bros., American International, 20th Century-Fox, Allied Artists, Columbia Pictures, Cinema Century Films, and Frederick O'Neal. I should also like to thank the Schomburg and Countee Cullen branches of the New York Public Library; the Theatre and Film Collection of the New York Public Library; and the Museum of Modern Art Film Library. And special thanks to Eric Benson, John Cocchi, Herb Graff, Dr. Frank Manchel, Chris Nelson, and Mark Ricci and his Memory Shop.

   G.N.

First Carol Publishing Group Edition 1990

Copyright © 1975 by Gary Null
A Citadel Press Book
Published by Carol Publishing Group

Editorial Offices
600 Madison Avenue
New York, NY 10022

Sales & Distribution Offices
120 Enterprise Avenue
Secaucus, NJ 07094

In Canada: Musson Book Company
A division of General Publishing Co. Limited
Don Mills, Ontario

Manufactured in the United States of America
ISBN 0-8065-0908-2

10 9 8 7 6 5

Contents

PUBLISHERS' NOTE

Black performers have appeared in Hollywood films for as long as motion pictures have been produced. In the early years the employment of black actors was rare, and when featured roles came along where a black player was required, the film's producer frequently hired a white actor and let him (or her) portray the part daubed with burnt cork.

This book is the record of the progress of the black artist from those early films to the present day, when some of the artists have become major stars and many films are devoted exclusively to black themes.

In a volume covering the number of players and films which this book attempts, it is very possible that some performers have been overlooked or given shorter shrift than an individual reader might think is deserved. Films, as well, which some readers may feel deserve attention may have been dwelt upon only briefly or not at all. One volume cannot, of course, do full justice to so vast a project.

This volume offers a cross-section of the forward movement of the black actor through three-quarters of a century of Hollywood films the author regards as best exemplifying this progress.

Chapter 1
Pre World War I to the Twenties

The influence of the screen for good or evil cannot be overestimated. As a propaganda medium it is the most powerful of agents. Napoleon said he feared one newspaper more than a thousand bayonets.

—WILLIAM PERLMAN
The Movies on Trial

Motion pictures are one of the most influential means of communication ever developed—a potentially powerful medium of propaganda. Hollywood, whose name is still synonymous with the vast commercial film industry in the United States, has denied this, claiming that films were merely entertainment; and Hollywood has never been known for progressive social attitudes.

The major studios have rarely done more than reflect and reinforce "safe" popular attitudes. This is nowhere more apparent than in the treatment of race. In particular, the depiction of black people on the screen has not only reinforced and sharpened some of the prejudices of the white majority, but it has also to a great extent shaped the often negative image blacks have had of themselves.

The original "Negro" performers were not black at all, but whites in blackface makeup. This tradition, which originated in the old slave days when white performers in the popular "nigger" minstrel shows blackened their faces with burnt cork to impersonate Negroes, was still the rule in the early days of the film industry. In 1905, white actors in blackface had already been on the stage for fifty years, portraying blacks as

foolish, childlike creatures, dancing around a fire and making fools of themselves to entertain their white masters. Negroes were considered incapable of playing themselves—or, to be more precise, of portraying the white images of themselves, which more polished white actors could do so much better. And who indeed could bring to life the stereotyped white conception of the Negro more accurately than a white actor in blackface?

This point in history saw the exodus of many disenfranchised Southern blacks to Northern cities in search of better economic opportunities. There were high hopes for social change when Teddy Roosevelt was elected president in 1904. Within a month of taking office, Roosevelt invited Booker T. Washington to the White House, and their conference resulted in the appointment of black men to governmental posts.

However, for the ordinary black worker, any change was for the worse. The white Northern industrialists did not want to employ Negroes, often refusing to hire them because of objections raised by white workers. Blacks seeking employment were intimidated and frequently beaten or lynched as the result of trumped-up charges brought against them by white workers. This era saw the beginning of race riots and the birth of the urban ghetto.

In 1905, W. E. B. DuBois spoke eloquently of the situation of the American Negro, stating:

> In the past fifty years the work of the Negro hater has flourished in the land. Step by step the defenders of the rights of American citizens have retreated. The work of stealing the Black man's ballot has progressed and the fifty or more representatives of stolen votes still sit in the nation's capital. . . . Never before in the modern age has a great and civilised folk threatened to adopt so cowardly a creed in the treatment of its fellow citizens, born and bred on its soil. Stripped of verbose subterfuge and in its naked nastiness, the new American creed says: Fear to let Black men even try to rise lest they become the equals of whites. . . .

The attitude reflected on the screen in the early days of silent films was that the blacks were stupid, lazy, clownishly inefficient, and quite incapable of performing even the most menial jobs if white workers needed them. Whites hotly debated the issue of black inferiority at the turn of the century, but even liberal whites cloaked their attitudes in paternalistic jargon. On the whole, Northerners disagreed with extremist Southern solutions to the race problem, but the Northern response to Ku Klux Klan activities indicated that even Northerners considered white supremacy only logical. Black people were generally considered temperamentally and physically inferior, labeled with such words as "childlike" and "bestial."

In 1902, an all-white cast performed George Méliès' *Off to Bloomingdale Asylum*. Here is Méliès' own description.

> An omnibus drawn by an extraordinary mechanical horse is actually pulled by four Negroes. The horse kicks and throws down the Negroes. As they fall they turn into white clowns. They begin slapping each other's faces and turn black again. Kicking each other, they become white once more. Suddenly they emerge into one gigantic Negro. When he refuses to pay carfare, the conductor sets fire to the omnibus and the Negro bursts into smithereens.

If we analyze this script in its socio-historical context, we might say that the mechanical horse, the work of which is really done by four Negroes, could symbolize the way whites saw the black man as a workhorse with little or no understanding of anything remotely complex. There is the explicit notion that blacks really wanted to be white but that their aping of white behavior was so ridiculous that it would betray them however hard they tried to "pass." In the symbol of the four's emergence into one giant Negro might lurk the Caucasian fear of black power. However, when the huge black man attempts to assert himself by refusing to pay carfare, he is quickly defeated. He is blown to smithereens, and white supremacy is saved.

Whether or not this interpretation accurately reflects Méliès' intentions, the racism in the film is blatant.

In film after film, the same Negro stereotypes appear—the foolish and irresponsible citizen, the grinning bellhop or flapjack cook, the hymn-singing churchgoer, the song-and-dance man, the devoted servant or contented slave, the barefoot watermelon eater, the corrupt politician, the hardened criminal, and the African savage. Thus emerge two broad categories into which the Negro can be fitted—the clown and the black brute.

In 1907 a film called *The Masher* was presented to the public as a "genuine comedy." In this film, a young man fails in his attempts to play the role of a Don Juan. None of the ladies he attempts to charm fall for his line. He finally meets with success when a lady wearing a veil responds to him. Pleased with his luck, he lifts the lady's veil and discovers, to his horror, that she is black. A Keystone Kop-like chase ensues, with our hero running amok in his attempt to escape from his conquest. This film and another entitled *The Wooing and Wedding of a Coon* (1905), filmed in four days, which mocked a black marriage, were successful enough to inspire many imitations.

Between 1909 and 1911, Sigmund Lubin produced the *Sambo* series of all-black comedies. This series was so successful that Lubin created a second and similar series, the *Rastus* films, about 1910. Both sets of films portrayed, with much slapstick, the antics of a comic black man who "knows his place" and gets the hell beat out of him by a variety of laughing whites.

Between 1910 and 1915 many similar films were made, including adaptations of Edward Sheldon's play *The Nigger* and Dion Boucicault's play *The Octoroon*. On the subject of the depiction of people of mixed blood in film, noted film historian Peter Noble, in the *The Negro in Films,* says,

> In all the films made during this period dealing with octoroons and mulattoes the apparent

shame and degradation of being even the smallest degree non-white was exploited to the full, with the obvious implication that there was something practically sub-human in being black.

A somewhat more sophisticated film on this subject was the 1912 movie *The Debt,* in which the children born to the white wife and the octoroon mistress of a white man grow up, meet, and fall in love. On the eve of their wedding, they discover to their misery that they are brother and sister and therefore cannot be married. The film seems to indicate not only that any connection between black and white is doomed to failure and misery, but also that owing to their black blood, mulattoes and octoroons are innately inferior and can have no better fate.

The first film in which any sympathy was shown for the position of the Negro was *The Judge's Story* (1911). A Negro youth is saved from imprisonment by a judge's impassioned plea to his white jury. In this story, the question of the boy's actual innocence or guilt is irrelevant. The point is that the boy's mother had once done the judge a favor. For the judge, saving the son is a way in which he can relieve his conscience of an unpaid debt. In *The Coward,* a film with Charles Ray, a white community's wrath is appeased by a Negro minister. Of course, this is possible only because he has God on his side.

While Hollywood seemed to be making minute progress in its attitudes to black-white relations at this time, blacks were just beginning to organize themselves to work for enforcement of the fourteenth and fifteenth amendments to the U.S. Constitution, complete enfranchisement of the Negro, abolition of enforced segregation, and equal education for black children. The National Association for the Advancement of Colored People (NAACP) was formed in 1910. Under its aegis, black and white lawyers worked together to overturn court decisions and use the courts in the fight to make Negroes full citizens. The National Urban League was established in 1911, with emphasis on opening new opportunities for Negroes in industry and assisting blacks newly arrived from the South with the problems they encountered in Northern urban centers. These groups had to battle constantly against all the forces of prejudice that tried to keep blacks "in their place."

Hollywood at this time certainly took no stand on social reform, being concerned, above all else, with profits. If a softening of attitudes did take place, it was almost imperceptible. Very much to the point is the fact that with very few exceptions, black characters were played by whites in all Hollywood films until after the First World War. The most famous of these blackface actors was Walter Long, who, during his long career, appeared in over fifty films, including *The Birth of a Nation, Soul Fire, Moby Dick,* and *The Maltese Falcon.*

In 1914 a black actor named Sam Lucas was given the title role in the third remake of *Uncle Tom's Cabin,* the first Hollywood film on a black theme to cast some Negro actors in black roles.

The first version of *Uncle Tom's Cabin* was produced as a one-reeler in 1903. Harriet Beecher Stowe's great abolitionist work, written as a passionate indictment of slavery, had attempted to portray blacks as human beings. The film, on the other hand, changed the story into a sentimental melodrama in which Uncle Tom was presented as a paragon of black subservience. The main emphasis of the film was on Uncle Tom's devotion for Little Eva, the invalid child of his white master. *Uncle Tom's Cabin* was remade yet again in 1918, this time with a white actress doubling as both Topsy and Eva and with most of the action revolving around the two girls.

In the meantime, a handful of independent "colored" film companies was emerging. These companies were owned by whites but catered exclusively to filmgoers in the nearly 400 black movie theaters, most of which were in the South. A major problem in producing these films was finance. An independent producer was rarely financed without joining forces with a major studio and drawing upon its artistic and financial resources. This meant that the black community was dependent on Hollywood unless backers could be found for large-scale productions or unless black producers learned to improvise.

One black producer who made films with a minimum of capital on very short shooting schedules was Oscar Micheaux, a wheeler-dealer who filmed *The Wages of Sin* and *The Broken Violin* in 1914 and *Harlem after Midnight* in 1934. Lacking a financial backer, Micheaux drove to every town in the South that either had a black cinema or had a theater that allowed blacks in one day a week. He would show the cinema managers still photographs of what he claimed was his latest film, "packing them in" in the North. The photographs might depict Lorenzo Tucker, his leading black male star, embracing a nude woman, or perhaps they would show a Harlem dance review. Micheaux asked the managers to advance him twenty dollars, and he would send him the film. Most of the

(Above) The first *Uncle Tom's Cabin*,
produced by Thomas A. Edison (1903).

(Below) Little Eva's apparition appears in the
same film.

cinema managers apparently fell for this technique and advanced him the money. In about a month, Micheaux would have enough money to finance a film.

Micheaux was unable to use studio lots for shooting his films, so again he improvised. He shot scenes in his own apartment, in Central Park, in the street. He wrote the scripts, directed the films, set up the lighting, edited the material, and handled his own distribution.

He used every exploitationary gimmick he could muster to grab the audience; for example, displaying large photos of rape scenes with seminude figures. He would insert sequences quite unrelated to the story into the films. Once he even inserted a scene of a Harlem dance troupe into a Western movie. The audiences loved the nudity and voiced their approval to the theater managers.

However, films attempting to deal with racial injustice were not being made by independent producers, black or white. Their emphasis, like that of the larger film industry, was on entertainment. This policy was not simply attributable to the profit motive, however. The feelings in the South toward blacks would have made it extremely dangerous to show any film to a black audience in which the social or political aspects of racism were depicted. Even though white audiences did not patronize black productions, had such a film been shown, the exhibiting movie house would have been burned down after no more than one performance. Most of the early black films were inferior even to Hollywood B movies and made on even more limited budgets.

If it seemed impossible for black producers to make anything but "safe" movies, their failure to utilize the talents of blacks in the technical aspects of filmmaking was a serious oversight. There have been few black screenwriters, directors, set designers, or film editors. The failure of the black producers in this respect may indicate that they were less concerned with the technical side of filmmaking than with acting. It must not be forgotten, however, that the technical trade unions were closed to blacks. Also, black producers and actors who worked for the independent companies were blackballed by their union leaders.

The social and political situation for blacks in the period before the First World War was bleak. By 1912, Negroes had become suspicious of Roosevelt, whose handling of the Brownsville incident had disappointed earlier hopes. Nor was any confidence placed in Taft, who had been elected president in 1908. NAACP officials therefore drafted a statement that they wished included in the progressive Republican platform. It

Bert Williams, the first major black star to appear in films (1914).

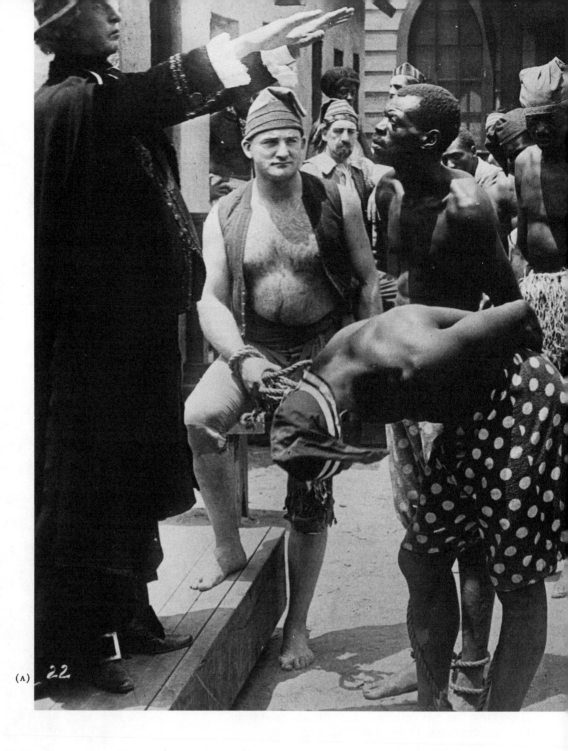

(A) 22

called once more for complete enfranchisement of all Negroes and pleaded for an end to unfair laws that discriminated against black and colored people in employment, housing, and other areas of life.

But Democrat Woodrow Wilson, who became president, was concerned primarily with banking and with tariff and trust reforms. Under his administration, the Clayton Anti-Trust Act was passed. This act sought to reform the industrial labor unions, but it did nothing for blacks, since most of them were excluded from the unions. In fact, Wilson's first congress was flooded with bills advocating discriminatory legislation against Negroes, and a Wilson executive order segregated eating and restroom facilities for federal employees.

In 1915 the president ordered the occupation of Haiti in the face of widespread black protests against the violation of that country's sovereignty and the killing of several hundred Haitians, which took place before peace was restored. It is perhaps significant that this was the year in which *The Birth of a Nation* was released.

D. W. Griffith's innovative film, a spectacular

(B)

(C)

(A) A slave auction. (B) Colonel Cameron (Henry B. Walthall) being denied the right to vote. (C) Walthall refuses to shake the hand of the mulatto leader (George Siegman) while Lillian Gish approves. (D) The typical Southern "mammy" berates the free Northern black.

(D)

Anita Bush, shown here in a 1917 publicity pose, was considered by critics to be the finest black actress of her era.

milestone in film history from the point of view of technical skill and acting, was also more detrimental to black people than any previous film.

The movie was based on the book *The Clansman*, by Thomas Dixon, whose writing was characteristically racist. Griffith, himself a Southerner, was labeled a bigot because his lofty theory of a universal moral order rested on an established white supremacy. Not only are blacks seen as inferior in this film, but many of the black characters are presented as decadent, brutal savages.

Briefly, the film deals with a family of South Carolina gentlefolk, the Camerons. Scenes of their idyllic pastoral existence include sequences of happy, contented slaves. The war changes this peaceful scene to one of horror, which intensifies with Reconstruction. "Uppity niggers" from the North, aided and abetted by the evil carpetbaggers, move into Piedmont, the home of the Cameron family. The old slaves are easily corrupted by the newcomers, and once they are stripped of the influence of their white former masters their innate brutality, in which Griffith evidently believed, comes to the surface in scenes of sadism, drunkenness, and lawless riot. The blacks (most played by white actors and actresses) are shown arrogantly abusing the whites in their attempt to take over the government of the old South. Following scenes depict the Negro's total inability to hold power, and the film expressively exploits the myth of the degenerately sensual black brute who lusts shamelessly after the pure white flower of Southern womanhood.

The culmination of the film shows the formation of the Ku Klux Klan, as white-robed figures led by that noble son of the South, Ben Cameron. In an impressive scene, the Klan rides to do battle with the blacks and defend white honor and white womanhood. They are victorious in this battle, and it is understood that they will also be victorious in their effort to restore to the South its trampled-on values, which will return peace and order.

Even in 1915 this film was condemned outright for its racism and not only by the NAACP and the black community. The glorification of the KKK caused much anxiety among the film's critics, who believed that it provided influential propaganda for the Klan. The movie was in fact banned in several states. Several rabidly anti-Negro films later tried to imitate *The Birth of a Nation*'s style, as well as its profits; however, the controversy over the Griffith film made it obvious that such racism was neither a wise nor a profitable subject for films. Nonetheless, *The Birth of a Nation*'s depiction of the Negro reinforced a trend that would not be broken for several decades.

There was, however, an exception. This was *Our Gang*, a series of comedies about the adventures of a

The Norman Film Mfg. Co. Presents the

CRIMSON SKULL

Baffling Western Mystery Photo~Play

THE CRIMSON SKULL.   ALL COLORED CAST.

CO-STARRING

ANITA BUSH and LAWRENCE CHENAULT

Supported by **BILL PICKETT**, World's Champion Wild West Performer, the one-legged Marvel, **STEVE REYNOLDS** and 30 Colored Cowboys.
Produced in the All-Colored City of Boley, Okla.

AN EPIC OF WILD LIFE AND SMOKING REVOLVERS

ALL-COLORED CAST | SIX SMASHING REELS

Miss Bush trussed up in a Western (circa 1920).

Farina and Our Gang in the 1920's

(A)

(B)

(C)

(A) Farina (Allen Clayton Hoskins) as he looked at the height of his *Our Gang* success. (B) Farina. (C) With his mother. (D) Left to right: Sunshine Sammy Morrison, Jay R. Smith, Farina, Mickey Daniels, Joe Cobb.

group of children, innovated by producer Hal Roach in 1918. The original cast included Farina as the pickaninny. This black boy became one of the most popular child stars in Hollywood. Instead of being a foil—or a slave—to the white kids, he stood on equal terms with them, was as much a part of the gang as the others.

In *The Negro in Films*, Peter Noble refers to some of the positive aspects of this series.

> For a large number of Hollywood films with a very wide appeal to indicate dozens of times, in a series lasting over a number of years, that there is no serious objection to white and coloured children playing together, seems to me to be a significant point.

(D)

The First World War had recently ended, and the fact that Negro soldiers had fought in it may have contributed to a softening of the white attitude towards blacks for at least a short while. But whereas a sympathetic depiction of black adults on the screen might have been too controversial, small white and colored children could safely be shown playing together without offending the *status quo*. In a sense, too, all the children in *Our Gang* were clowns, and this was one of the major roles permitted to the Negro. In the next decade, with the advent of talking pictures, the voice of the Negro, talking and singing, would most distinguished him and her from white society.

Chapter 2
The Late Twenties

Between me and the other world there is ever
an unasked question: unasked by some through
a feeling of delicacy; by others through the
difficulty of rightly framing it. All, nevertheless
flutter round it. They approach me in a half-
hesitant sort of way, eye me curiously or
compassionately, and then, instead of saying
directly, How does it feel to be a problem?
They say, I know an excellent colored man in
my town; or, I fought at Mechanicsville; or,
Do not these Southern outrages make your
blood boil? At these I smile, or am interested,
or reduce the boiling to a simmer, as the
occasion may require. To the real question,
How does it feel to be a problem? I answer
seldom a word.

—W. E. B. DU BOIS
The Souls of Black Folks (1903)

In the late twenties, talking pictures became the
newest Hollywood sensation, changing the medium of
film forever. Film became "realistic" in a way that the
theater could never be. Movies had accustomed the
public to seeing places to which the stage could only
allude; and whereas the theater audience had to supply
much of the action from its imagination, the cinema
was explicit. Once directors had begun to realize the
potential of sound as used in film, the scope of the
medium was tremendously enlarged. To quote André
Malraux,

The sound film changed the state of the film
medium, although not, as some say, by
"perfecting" the silent film. The sound film is
no more a perfecting of the silent film than
the elevator is a perfecting of the skyscraper.
. . . As long as sound in films remained merely
phonographic it was as pointless as the silent
film was while it remained photographic. It
became an art when the directors understood
that the ancestor of sound in talking films
was not the phonograph record but radio
techniques.

Again:

The inspiration of contrast [that is,
juxtaposition of sound and image] becomes a
perfecting; then the sound film becomes to
the silent film what painting is to sketching.

Whatever technological and artistic advantages
might lie ahead, the greatest sociological importance of
film, and thus its power, lay in its popular appeal. The
stage catered only to the more affluent sectors of society,
but the cinema reached, and was able to influence, a far
wider public.

During the late 1920s, the film industry began to
realize that movies should present a realistic picture of
life as it was lived by the whole of society, not just part
of it. Film, it was recognized, had more in common
with the novel than with the stage play and was suited
to presenting the same panoramic view of society.
Perhaps this attitude was what brought black actors and
actresses into films during the early days of the talkies.
Of course, the NAACP agitated for an end of blackface
roles, but the Association was young and relatively

Will Rogers, Irene Rich in *Boys Will Be Boys* (1921). Unidentified actress is in blackface.

ZaSu Pitts in blackface in *Pretty Ladies* (1925). Joan Crawford appeared in this.

Porter Strong in blackface in D.W. Griffith's *One Exciting Night* (1922).

Rosetta and Vivian Duncan as *Topsy and Eva.*

powerless. Nevertheless, a few blacks had earned parts in the silent films and as the talkies took over, the black voice became heard more and more.

However, the first official talking film significantly enough featured Al Jolson, the popular white singer, in blackface. This, of course, was *The Jazz Singer* of 1927, which carried the tradition of the old "nigger" minstrel show into a new technological age. Although it is to Jolson's credit that he lent some dignity to his role, the blackface tradition had always been basically demeaning to Negroes.

It is significant that even when the minstrel shows had been opened to black performers, allowed to tour as members of all-black companies, the tradition had continued, and Negro performers had frequently been expected to blacken their faces with burnt cork—an effective reinforcement of their essentially self-mocking roles.

As Ralph Ellison pointed out in *The Invisible Man*, whites frequently do not "see" blacks as human beings or especially as "real Americans." Negroes' self-conception has been deeply influenced by this

attitude. The judgment of the Supreme Court, in the case of *Plessy* versus *Ferguson* in 1896, said,

> Our constitution is color-blind, and neither knows nor tolerates classes among citizens. In respect of civil rights, all citizens are equal before the law. The humblest is the peer of the most powerful. The law regards man as man, and takes no account of his color when his civil rights guaranteed by the supreme law of the land are involved.

But to both white and black society, this judgment might never have existed. "The problem of the Twentieth Century," stated DuBois, "is the problem of the color line."

In the twenties and thirties this problem showed itself in a perverse way. During this period white men often played the then famous "boogie" game, a drawing-room version of the minstrel shows, in which participants would blacken their faces and affect their versions of Negro dialect. And these exaggerated white versions of the Negro voice were popularized by the cinema in the same way that white versions of Negro personality had been presented in the silent films.

(Left) Rosetta Duncan with Noble Johnson in the *Uncle Tom's Cabin* version entitled *Topsy and Eva* (1927).

Lorenzo Tucker, hailed as the black Valentino (1927).

Al Jolson in blackface in *The Jazz Singer* (1927).

There were some changes in the way in which the white majority viewed blacks, and almost imperceptible as they were, these changes were reflected in the films. For one thing, the image of the screen Negro as a total villain, as in *The Birth of a Nation*, was no longer credible. The image of black people in the films of the twenties, the early talkie era, was sentimentalized and softened. More important, perhaps, although the image was set by whites, it was being portrayed more and more by black actors. Still, the roles were essentially blackface roles, the only difference being that blacks were taking them over.

Al Jolson was by no means the last white performer to play a blackface role, but in his swooning rendition of "Mammy" and other songs he represented a dying tradition. Also, he brought some credibility to

his part, which he played with understanding and sympathy. This "darkie" was approaching humanity and possessed a quality of dignity that would rarely be allowed to blacks on screen until Poitier in the sixties made it acceptable.

Others tried to imitate Jolson and failed. Nor were blacks necessarily much more successful in portraying the roles they were given than were white actors in blackface. The early days of the talkies, so ruinous to many a silent actor's career, affected blacks too, because the speech expected of black actors was essentially the dialect of the Southern shanties. One example of this was black child actor Farina, of *Our Gang*. Farina had been born in Boston and schooled in stagecraft, and his perfect enunciation so horrified the director that he was quickly shuffled off to

(A) Virginia Grey as Eva with Marie Foster. (B) George Siegmann as Simon Legree. James B. Lowe (on the floor) is Uncle Tom. (C) James B. Lowe and Virginia Grey. (D) Virginia Grey with her father (John Roche), James B. Lowe and Adolph Milar as the slave trader.

Scenes from
Uncle Tom's Cabin
(1927)

(D)

(C)

desophisticate his language. Unhappy with individual performers who did not sound as if they had just wandered off a plantation, directors turned to groups. For instance, a "novelty" revue band called the Jubilee Singers gained great popularity with their melodic vocal qualities and their use of primitive instruments. They appeared in the 1927 version of *Uncle Tom's Cabin.*

The late twenties and the thirties saw the growing popularity of the black song-and-dance man, and it became well known that Negroes had "natural rhythm." Certainly there was a wealth of musical and dancing talent among the blacks who had recently arrived in the Northern urban centers from the South, and this the Hollywood producers were quick to tap.

In 1929, Fox Films presented *Hearts in Dixie*, the first vehicle for this natural-rhythm-of-the-blacks mystique. Billed as the first all-singing, all-dancing, all-Negro musical, it was so popular that many more were to follow. But as the pioneer film of this genre, *Hearts in Dixie* did nothing for the Negro image. Although Mordaunt Hall in *The New York Times* called the film

(Left) Stepin Fetchit's first film, *In Old Kentucky* (1927). (Above) Stepin Fetchit

restful, a talking and singing production that is gentle in its mood and truthful in its reflection of the black men in those days down yonder in the cornfields,

Peter Noble, in *The Negro in Films*, disagreed:

We were given no new slant on Negro life and thought, just the same old hackneyed routine. The story was so slight as to be almost non-existent, but apparently we were to be compensated for this by a succession of endless musical numbers, spirituals, prayer meetings, cotton picking and the like.

In the story line, which was apparently added after the Fox people had worked out a plot to go with the musical numbers, an old black man sacrifices his life for his son. The characters were two dimensional cardboard cutouts of black slaves toiling on the plantation for their benevolent white masters, singing spirituals while they picked bales and bales of cotton and spending their evenings with more singing, dancing, and praising the Lord. The three main roles brought to the screen the talents of Clarence Muse, Mildred Washington, and Stepin Fetchit. Clarence Muse played the father, and Stepin Fetchit led the songs and played the very incarnation of the irresponsible nigger who knew his place, loved his master, and just grinned for joy every time his laziness was rewarded by a kick in the pants.

Scenes from
Hearts In Dixie
(1929)

(A)

(A) (Left to Right) Clifford Ingram, Mildred Washington and Eugene Jackson. (B) Stepin Fetchit and Clarence Muse. (C) Stepin Fetchit and Bernice Pilot.

(B)

(C)

Such crazy antics, in this and other films, made Stepin Fetchit one of the most famous black actors.

In the happy fantasy world of *Hearts in Dixie*, there were no beatings or killings, such as actually occurred on the plantations. The film was touted by the studio as "a major triumph" and dismissed by many critics as a failure, its message, if one had cared to read it, was just as clear as in D. W. Griffith's violently racist films: To keep the world from floundering in chaos, "social order" must be maintained—that is, the dumb niggers must be kept in their place.

Henry Dobbs, in *Close Up*, wrote,

Specifically, we might have advanced since the

Daniel L. Haynes, hand on forehead, Fannie Belle De Knight, Harry Gray.

mountebankery of Griffith's *One Exciting
Night* though Stepin Fetchit's roles in *The
Ghost Talks* and *Hearts in Dixie* are directly
in the tradition of the vaudeville stage and the
blackface comics. The Negro, in short, for all
his humanity, is still behind the bars of his
cage, a cage flooded with the glare of publicity
and intoned with "the haunting strains of
Negro spirituals." It is obvious from *Hearts
in Dixie* that director Paul Sloane has not
yet emerged from that state of mind which
conceives of the Negro film as leaning towards
open-necked shirts, banana hats, and the
melodic charms of "Old Black Joe" and "The
Lonesome Road." The tragedy is not the
tragedy *in* the film but the tragedy *of* the film:
the tragedy of these untainted folk, strutting
their stuff to the required pattern, playing their
parts as the white man likes to believe they
are. The Negro and his colored brothers are
not museum pieces. Nor are they mountebanks.
If they are blessed with more than human
power of music and speech, of rhythm and
color, then they have it over us whites. But if
Hearts in Dixie is a specimen of colored
expression under the aegis of Hollywood, let
us, next time, hand the whole process over to
the Negroes themselves.

King Vidor (with megaphone) and
the Dixie Jubilee Singers.

Hearts in Dixie was resounding box-office success. One critic called it "the biggest box-office attraction in the history of all-Negro films." Other major studios were quick to follow up with similar movies, competing with each other to sign up black musical-comedy talent for such movies as *Shuffle Along, Blackbirds,* and *Hallelujah.* These movies made the careers of several very talented black actors who were assured of a long chain of similar roles, so long as they did not attempt to break the restrictions of type-casting.

MGM's offering was the 1929 film *Hallelujah,* billed as the "ace of all-black pictures" and employing the talents of the studio's ace director, King Vidor. *Hallelujah,* like *Hearts in Dixie,* was a spectacular film with more than forty singing and dancing sequences including folk songs, spirituals, work songs, and blues. Unlike *Hearts in Dixie,* this film had a strong plot; the message, however, was the same—blacks should know their place.

The place of the black family portrayed in *Hallelujah* was down on the farm picking cotton. Some

progress had been made, however, for now the family were sharecroppers; this was not the white man's plantation. The film kept the situation safe by excluding white people from the action. The problems that beset the idyllic family existence of the story came as a result of the base nature that, the film seems to assume, is innate in Negroes but can be kept in check.

This nature, irrevocably linked to sexuality, is brought out when the youngest son of the family goes to town and meets the character known as "Chick," a cabaret dancer played by the light-skinned Negro actress Nina Mae McKinney, who was later billed as "the screen's first black love goddess." The male lead, played by Daniel Haynes, rapidly yields to temptation, is led to squander his family's hard-earned money, and accidentally kills his brother in a brawl. However, he repents, spectacularly.

His repentance gives the studio an opportunity to introduce scenes of religious fervor as Haynes becomes a preacher. A full-scale revival meeting culminates in a river baptism as Haynes leads McKinney to religion. Not for long though. Almost immediately the young

William Fountaine admires Nina Mae McKinney doing Irving Berlin's "Swanee Shuffle" while Daniel L. Haynes looks on.

Daniel L. Haynes with Everett McGarrity.

preacher deserts his congregation for a life of
corruption with the woman who in turn betrays him. In
a fit of jealousy he kills her and her lover, and this
crime of passion apparently frees him from his moral
fall to return home, once more repentant, to the bosom
of his family and the good black girl he left behind
him.

The white reaction to *Hallelujah* is reflected in the
comments of the supposedly sophisticated *Times* critic
Mordaunt Hall, whose attitude testifies to his racism:

> The humor that issues from *Hallelujah* is
> natural unto the Negro, whether it deals with
> hankering after salvation, the dread of water in
> baptism, the lure of the "come seven, come
> 'leven" or the belated marital ceremonies. . . .
> the ways of the dusky sons of Ham. . . .
> The audience was much amused by the
> scenes dealing with the baptism of the darkies,

34

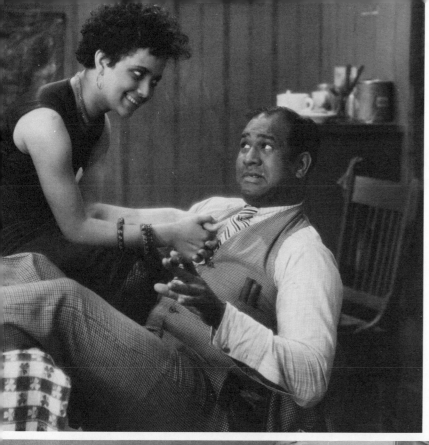

(Left) Nina Mae McKinney and William Fountaine.

(Below) Victoria Spivey (far left), Fannie Belle De Knight and Daniel L. Haynes.

Nina Mae McKinney and Fannie Belle De Knight.

especially the first and second immersions. . . .
He finally succumbs to her peculiar
fascination, jilting a girl as black as coal for
the chocolate colored Chick.

The conflict in this highly melodramatic film
suggests a confrontation between good and evil
embodied in the two basic Negro stereotypes—the
savage brute and the humble and subservient buffoon.

The depiction of women in the film follows a
pattern that has only recently been broken.
Dark-skinned women were seen as sexless; they were
usually fat, good-natured servant figures such as would
become well known in the thirties as played by actresses
like Hattie McDaniel and Louise Beavers. Only
light-skinned black women who represented a basically
white style of beauty were shown as sexually desirable.
The character portrayed by Nina Mae McKinney in
Hallelujah is seen as having no moral character at all,
and this again is typical. In films, as in "real life,"
those of too obviously mixed blood were especially the
objects of contumely.

Of particular interest, also, is that there are no
grave consequences for Haynes for the violent acts he
commits. The murders result, not in the dreadful
punishment of the law, but in repentance and release.
The film is saying that violence and criminality are
integral parts of the Negro's nature, and so long as the
victim is not white, retribution is unnecessary. This
offhand attitude toward black violence is recurrent in

Negro movies, a case in point being Porgy's escape
from responsibility for his killing of Bess's man in
Porgy and Bess.

At the end of the twenties the NAACP was young
and not particularly influential, as yet very timid in its
demands. The Association could perhaps take some
satisfaction from knowing that black roles were being
taken over by blacks. But the stereotypes, though
softened and often sentimentalized, were firmly in
place. Stepin Fetchit in particular was attacked by fellow
blacks for what they regarded as his highly lucrative
betrayal of his race. He made famous a character that
represented the worst aspects of the servant
archetype—the comically incompetent idiot whose head
scratching, eye rolling, and shuffling were the constant
butt of more or less tolerantly superior whites. This
"good nigger" was attacked by angry black journalists
all over the United States. He replied to their
accusations with the remark that he was "just trying to
make a living."

"Some way to make a living," retorted a black
editor.

Clarence Muse, another famous black actor, also
benefited from his secure place in Hollywood, earning
"a salary so high as to be ridiculous"; yet Muse held a
quite different attitude. He saw in his success a chance
to advance the status of blacks, and he became a prime
mover in the attempt to improve the lot of black actors.
He also attempted to improve the black image by
cleaning up the scripts he was given. He said,

Nina Mae McKinney.

Bessie Smith in her only film, *St. Louis Blues* (1928).

Bessie Smith.

Jonquil and Permanent Williams in *Melancholy Dame* (1929).

The setup in Hollywood is highly commercial, and I don't believe that the film city is in any sense truly creative. I think they reach out for successful books, plays, even people, to build up their great industry, and in the material which they buy, the Negro is invariably a stereotype.

Hollywood would buy and make a best-selling book . . . even if it featured a Negro as the central character, if the book were successful enough. I don't think politics enters into the question at all. . . . As soon as better material . . . becomes popular with the mass American public, then Hollywood will follow the trend. . . .

The actor is the highly finished tool of the author. What we need are more Negro authors and screenwriters. . . . The Negro has lived in a world of conflict and struggle for generations and of such influences are sublime works created

Unfortunately, Muse either failed to realize or refused to perceive that the derogatory way in which Hollywood depicted black people was bound to perpetuate the vision whites had of blacks, as well as being detrimental to the blacks themselves. Hollywood, more than any other institution, helped to perpetuate racial bias by retaining a tradition of demeaning blacks, thus making a sort of negative political statement. If this was not so, why was it to be more than two decades before Hollywood hired its first Negro screenwriter? Why was Muse told to replace many lines he had rejected because of their racial slurs? Why did Muse apparently have to succumb to such demands?

The thirties were to see a building up of the modified black stereotypes of the late twenties, but this decade was also to see the beginnings of a radical change of consciousness among blacks. The thirties would bring great social upheavals, during which all sectors of society would begin to question hitherto accepted social values. To some degree, all this would be reflected by Hollywood.

Lorenzo Tucker and Ethel Moses in *Wages of Sin* (1928).

(Left) Ethel Waters sings "Am I Blue?" in
On With the Show (1929).

Advertising poster for Lorenzo Tucker's *The Black King* (1931).

Chapter 3
The Thirties

The box-office insistence that the Negro shall figure always as a clown has spoiled two Negro films which have been made in Hollywood, *Hallelujah* and *Hearts in Dixie*.

In *Hallelujah* they took the Negro and his church service and made them funny. . . . Hollywood can only visualize the plantation type of Negro . . . the Negro of "Poor Old Joe" and "Swanee Ribber." It is as absurd to use that type to express the modern Negro as it would be to express modern England in the terms of an Elizabethan ballad.

—PAUL ROBESON
writing in *Film Weekly*

The thirties was a decade of great social upheaval. The outstanding events of the period—the Wall Street crash, the Depression, and the outbreak in Europe of the Second War War, which the United States was soon to enter—had outstanding consequences for the entire nation. Yet the films of the period show little awareness that profound changes were occurring in the structure of American society.

At the beginning of the decade, Hollywood saw its role as providing escapist entertainment from the grim realities of the Depression. This approach had some validity, for audiences were not willing to see reflections of their own unhappiness on the screen. Films like *The Kid from Spain*, with Eddie Cantor, and Cecil B. DeMille's *The Sign of the Cross,* both made in 1932, gave moviegoers a few hours of pleasure. However, the film industry too, was affected by the Depression, and not surprisingly, the Negroes employed by the studios suffered most.

Blacks everywhere were the hardest hit of the underprivileged minorities. Their hard-won financial, social, and educational status, which had been gradually rising, fell to their lowest point since 1915. Unable to find work in the cities, blacks became migrant workers or tenant farmers. Black communities everywhere suffered great privation. Most blacks on the Hollywood casting roles were extras. As in other professions, the Negro actors were the last hired and the first fired.

Blacks cast in larger roles were often caught in an identity crisis. As the decade progressed, more and more blacks began to object to the roles they were forced to play. Others found themselves playing a number of roles not specifically Negro in order to work. Thus, for instance, Hazel Jones found herself playing a Burmese siren in *West of Singapore,* and Etta Moten played a dark-skinned South American in *Flying Down to Rio.* Most blacks who made it in the entertainment world were members of the middle and upper classes.

According to Gunnar Myrdal, author of *An American Dilemma,* these successful performers made many whites take another look at the black race, and their rise, Myrdal believed,

has made the whites more friendly and sometimes it has given them a measure of respect for Negroes. . . . Interest in the arts may have improved the taste and poise of Negroes; but interest in entertainment may have degraded their tastes. In a number of ways . . . entertainment and the arts have had a pervasive influence on practically all Negroes.

Whatever the truth of this, the black actors who became popular movie stars were still relegated to demeaning roles. Hollywood writers and directors may have been aware of the new black middle class, but the stock black characters were poor Southern shanty dwellers or comic servants. As black technician, composer, and band leader Phil Moore put it,

> Admittedly, when film producers show Negroes as maids and servants it is a true picture, but it is also true that there are Negro doctors and lawyers and soldiers, and I would like to see them on the screen once in a while too. Many better film parts have been written for Negroes but have subsequently been struck out because the producers do not think it is a commercial proposition to give Negroes good roles.

Hollywood producers were reluctant to make films that challenged the stereotypes, for controversial films endangered profits. To prove this point, they could cite the case of a film called *Arrowsmith*.

John Ford produced *Arrowsmith*, starring Ronald Colman and Helen Hayes, in 1931. Based on a novel by Sinclair Lewis, the film dealt with a struggle between ambition and dedication to human well-being. The principal character, Dr. Arrowsmith, played by Colman, struggles for recognition in the field of medicine but then sets fame aside and goes to a small Caribbean island to help fight an epidemic. He meets another doctor who, like himself, has for the moment set aside a career as a prominent doctor to assist the poor people of the island. Both doctors work together for what the film's publicity called the "common cause." The Caribbean doctor, played by Clarence Brooks, is black.

Critics believed that in casting Brooks in the role of the second doctor, a breakthrough had been made, not only in black casting, but in the overall depiction of

Cover of press book for *Daughter of the Congo* (1930).

Clarence Brooks, the black doctor in *Arrowsmith*, stands between Richard Bennett and Ronald Colman (1931).

Leading characters in the order of appearance:—Joe Byrd as WHERABOO—Katherine Noisette as LUPELTA, "A Daughter of the Congo"—Wilhelmina Williams as REESHA—Clarence Redd as LODANGO—Lorenzo Tucker as CAPTAIN PAUL DALE—Roland Irving as LIEUTENANT BROWN—Alice B. Russell as "MISS PATTIE"—Charles Moore as JOHN CALVERT—Gertrude Snelson as HIS SISTER—Percy Verwayn as PIDGLY MUFFY—Madame Robinson as LOBUE—Salem Tutt Whitney as KOJO, President of the Republic—Willor Lee Guilford as HULDA—"Speedy" Wilson as MWAMBA, etc., etc. THE SINGER—Daisy Harding. TAP DANCER, Rudolph Dawson

Another press release for *Daughter of the Congo*.

Negroes. Financially, however, the film did not make it. To Hollywood's money men, to whom the way Negroes were portrayed on the screen was chiefly a matter of profits, the financial failure of *Arrowsmith* showed only that racist films made far more money.

It took an independent producer to film *The Black King* in 1932. This film, an early study in black power, is about a man in control of the people with whom he surrounds himself. Like all government heads and most businessmen, the Black King works on the theory that he must hire only people who are intelligent but controllable. The film pointed out that there was as rigid a caste system within Negro society as within white society and that blacks do not need whites to run their lives. In the story, the blacks are independent of whites, although the King is in total control until the end, when he falls prey to his own tyranny.

Such a film would never have been produced by a major studio, but it is important in the history of independent black films and in the establishment of a black genre in the film industry. Such considerations did not interest the Hollywood moguls. Where was the profit in such a film?

To prove their point, producers could cite two other films that appeared in 1932 and were far more successful financially than *Arrowsmith* or *The Emperor Jones*, which would appear in 1933. Both films, *White Zombie* and *Kongo*, bore the clear message that there was an obvious distinction between the primitive barbarism of black ancestry and the cultured ancestry of whites. In neither film were the Negroes presented as real people; they were merely there for local flavor.

Victor Halperin's *White Zombie* is set in Haiti, where one of a bevy of evil necromancers, the rather picturesquely named Murder Legendre (Bela Lugosi), commands his flock of mindless but physically superb black zombies who obey his every order with frantic haste. Lugosi is involved in such ventures as hypnotizing blondes into killing their boyfriends, throwing butlers into subterranean streams, and releasing crazed eagles and vultures from the battlements of his mountaintop castle to go down and plague the islands. Protesters are thrown to their deaths in the moat below the castle by Lugosi's black follower-slaves.

The main tension of the plot is provided by the unsuccessful attempts of a sympathetic truck driver to escape the madness. Clarence Muse also had a role in this film.

Characters were given lines that had nothing to do with the plot. In fact, the film was so confused, so clumsy, that most interest centers on the background detail. This was provided by the exotically bestial behavior of the blacks as they engaged in various activities including, of course, voodoo rites. No attempt was even made to portray the voodoo rites realistically or sympathetically. The Negro chanters and dancers were shown as completely evil, with no regard for each other or themselves. All their activities were marked by savage screams and contorted, twisted faces. Their evil ways earned them early death.

When director Halperin was asked why he had cast the Negro characters in such unfavorable light, his answer was that his sole intention had been to show life in Haiti as it actually was. He claimed that he and his staff had spent several months researching rituals throughout the Caribbean and that the voodoo sequences in the film were in keeping with the study.

The other film, *Kongo*, with Walter Huston and Lupe Velez, is set in the Congo, where the primitive, drum-pounding tribesmen are only of incidental interest. Playing the main character, the trader Flint, Huston portrays an embittered misanthrope who, as the film continually stresses, has an excuse for every violent act he performs, whether beating his wife or killing a number of natives. Because his whole life has been a series of misfortunes, because he is a cripple, and because his face is covered with terrible scars, he is presented as a character deserving of compassion.

The white man's burden is the key theme of this film and the justification for Flint's warped existence in the heat of the African trading post. The audience is asked to sympathize with Flint as he commits acts of hatred such as shooting a native in the back. The blacks, on the other hand, are convenient objects upon whom Flint can vent his malice, caused by the treatment of a hostile world. They also provide the exotic background with their frenzied drumming and primitive dancing.

Hollywood not only disliked taking risks, but also helped maintain the negative black image by its failure to employ screenwriters capable of scripting films that dealt realistically with black life. Writing in the *Amsterdam News,* screenwriter Sada Cown said,

> As a scenarist working in the motion picture studios, I try to depict life realistically, at least as honestly as I can. I try to present people not as I should like to have them, but as they really are in the everyday walks of life. I try to paint them impartially without emotion.

She went on to talk of what she called "the higher type of Negro"—the lawyers, doctors, professional people—as being regarded by most whites of the time as "social freaks."

SEE THEM
-:-
Send Forth
"THE DECOY"
-:-
Arrange
"THE CONTACT"
-:-
Put a Squealer
"ON THE SPOT"

AN EPIDEMIC OF HIGH-YALLERS AND SUGAR-CURED BROWNS STRAIGHT FROM HARLEM AND SIZZLIN' YEAH HOT!! MAN

In a Story that is
Different!
-:-
Melodrama with
Music!

Gangdom in Action
Again — but from
a new angle — the
Angle of the Kid-
naper! . . . .

AN
OSCAR MICHEAUX
PRODUCTION
"Harlem
After Midnight"
WITH AN
ALL STAR COLORED CAST

(Above) Cover of a press book for Oscar Michaux's *Harlem After Midnight* (1934).

(Left) Still from an unreleased MGM
Joan Crawford film, *Great Day*. Gertrude
Howard is on the left (1930).

Stepin Fetchit entertains Gertrude Howard (left), in *Carolina* (1934).

Stepin Fetchit, Francis Ford and Will Rogers in *Steamboat Round the Bend* (1935).

(Left) Stepin Fetchit pleads with Will
Rogers in *Judge Priest* (1934).

(A)

(C)

(B)

(D)

Blackface in the 1930's

(E)

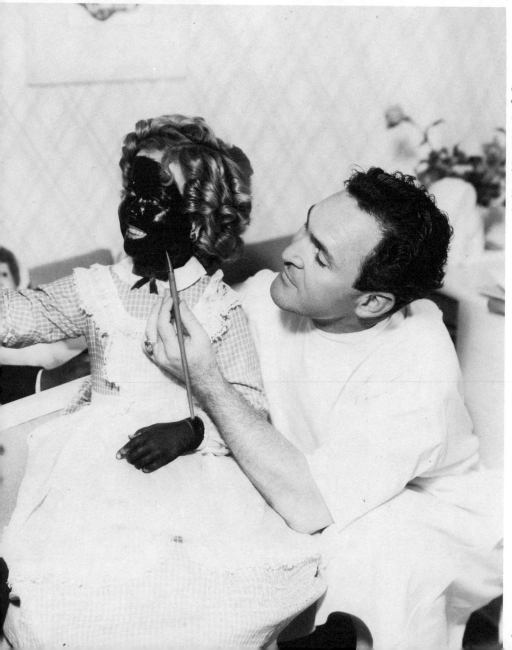

(A) Jimmy Durante with George M. Cohan in blackface in *The Phantom President* (1932). (B) Amos 'n' Andy (Freeman Gosden and Charles Correll in blackface) in *Check and Double Check* (1930). (C) Moran and Mack (The Two Black Crows) in *Anybody's War* (1930). (D) Making up. . . .Shirley Temple and Bill Robinson. (E) Marion Davies disguises herself as a mulatto in *Operator 13* with Sam McDaniel (1934).

(A)

(B)

(C)

(D)

(A) Paul Muni in *Seven Faces* (1929).
(B). Mickey Rooney and Judy Garland in
blackface in *Babes in Arms* (1939).
Douglas McPhail is between them. (C)
Edgar Bergen holds a blackfaced Charlie
McCarthy on his lap, while W. C. Fields
looks on, in *You Can't Cheat an Honest
Man* (1939). (D) Fred Astaire doing
"Bojangles of Harlem" in *Swingtime*
(1936).

To the black public, these "social freaks" were often regarded with hostility for having crossed over to the white side. Those who had moved up socially were often accused of playing Uncle Tom to their white masters.

Many blacks felt special resentment during the Depression when, in contrast to a background of economic crisis, while workers were laid off and hunger marchers gathered in Washington, D.C., a few black stars were living very well, by enacting roles that did nothing but harm to their race. During the Depression, the black press gave more space to the salaries of black stars than to nearly any other subject. In May 1933 Harry Levette, of the *Pittsburgh Courier*, said,

> In answer to many queries as to the salaries paid to "ours" in the movies, we found that

(A) Eddie Cantor in blackface in *Roman Scandals* (1933). (B) Judy Garland in blackface with Allan Jones in *Everybody Sing* (1938). (C) Al Jolson in blackface sings "Goin' to Heaven on a Mule" in *Wonder Bar* (1934).

(c)

(B)

none is getting as high as were James B. Lowe for *Uncle Tom's Cabin* or Stepin Fetchit for *Hearts in Dixie.*

James B. Lowe is said to be paid over a thousand dollars a week by his studio, and Stepin Fetchit $1500 a week by Fox Studios. The average black actor working today is paid $25 a day with few exceptions, such as Louise Beavers, Gertrude Howard, Charlie Moore and Oscar Smith, who receive between $25 and $50 a day. The pay for the extras fell the last year of the prolonged depression from $7.50 a day to $5.00.

Black actors, too, deplored the way in which fine actors like Stepin Fetchit and Bill Robinson sold out to Hollywood. Each of these stars earned more money than the combined salaries of fifty equally able actors and actresses, and they earned it by pandering to the most demeaning white myths about blacks. It was felt that they were more interested in living well at the expense of their race than in making any attempt to combat their typecasting. A radio commentator in the mid-thirties remarked bitterly,

> If Stepin wants to go on looking like a damned fool, rolling eyes and stuttering out ungrammatical and undecipherable inanities, and if Bill wants to go on clattering up and down stairs after a mincing Miss Temple . . . well, it *is* a free country. And look at the money they're puttting away for the later years. They'll hardly turn out to be any "Old Black Joe" figure of contempt.

Robinson's reply to such criticism was that he would never be given any roles at all if he refused those which were offered him. To him it was "as simple as that. I want to stay alive."

Fetchit's high salary reflected his box-office appeal in films like director John Ford's *Judge Priest* (1934), in which, as Jeff Poindexter, he played his usual "good darkie" character and won commendation such as that of Andre Sennwald, who reviewed the film for *The New York Times.*

> That cloudy streak of greased lightning, Stepin Fetchit, is riotous as the judge's man of all or no work, and he is always threatening to drop the auditors into Radio City's plush aisles.

This film, a situation comedy set in the years just following the Civil War, takes place on the archetypal Southern plantation of the movie world. It tells the story of a Kentucky judge who successfully manages to rescue a young nephew from the twin snares of a matchmaking mother and the county jail.

Shirley Temple, Bill Robinson and Willie Best in *The Littlest Rebel* (1935).

Will Rogers, in the title role of the judge who is both philosopher and gentleman, presides over a house filled with memories of his dead wife and child, surrounded by his faithful Negro retainers and his favorite items, corn whiskey and honeysuckle. A fine, simple man, he is as fond of his Negroes as they are devoted to him and is even able to join his washerwoman in song at a taffy pull.

The film received generally good reviews, but some critics attacked it for a lack of social responsibility. A critic in Newark, New Jersey, characterized *Judge Priest* as a film of great surface charm that bent over backward to evoke essentially negative nostalgic myths about the past.

Bill Robinson, better known as Mr. Bojangles, played Shirley Temple's darkie buddy in *The Little*

Colonel (1935), *The Littlest Rebel* (1935), and *Rebecca of Sunnybrook Farm* (1938). Bojangles presented a very different image from that of Stepin Fetchit. For example, in *The Littlest Rebel*, he was the solid, dependent, reliable servant who, as Miss Temple's trusted friend, could protect her when the Yankees invaded the plantation and carried her father, the colonel, off to prison.

Robinson's chief resource lay in his phenomenal ability as a tap dancer, and all his films featured this talent. In *One Mile from Heaven* (1937), he was a dance teacher. But although his personality was different from Fetchit's, his screen role was just as much that of a "good nigger." His permitted screen relationship with Shirley Temple showed the condescending blacks-are-just-like-little-children

(Above) Bill Robinson with unidentified player in *Café Metropole* (1937). (Right) Bill Robinson dances in *The Big Broadcast of 1936.*

attitude—and he never stepped out of line.

In *The Littlest Rebel,* Shirley Temple appears in blackface in one scene as she tries to hide from Yankee soldiers by disguising herself as a pickaninny. Blackface had not completely disappeared from the screen; Al Jolson appeared in this guise with black co-actors in *The Singing Kid* (1936).

A scene in *Modern Times,* a film about unemployment, says a great deal very briefly about the position of blacks in society and in Hollywood during the thirties. Seated in a paddy wagon on its way to jail is a patient colored woman. Every time the truck swerves Charlie Chaplin is unavoidably thrust onto her lap. Each time he falls on her, the woman gently pushes Chaplin away and straightens her skirt. She never loses her composure, and she plays her tiny part with a quiet

Bill Robinson

Scenes from
Imitation of Life
(1934)

(A)

(A) Louise Beavers and Claudette Colbert. (B) Miss Beavers with Fredi Washington. (C) Miss Beavers, Miss Colbert with, at far right, Madame Sul-te-Wan.

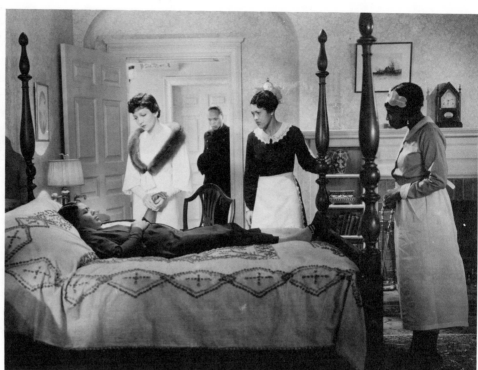

(c)

dignity that contrasts with Chaplin's antics.

The figure of this simple, humble black woman, so accepting of her lot, is a miniature of the type of character portrayed by Louise Beavers in *Imitation of Life* (1934), which created a storm of controversy. In this film, starring Claudette Colbert and Warren William, one of the principal themes involves a Negro girl trying to pass as white. Louise Beavers played the girl's mother, a black-mammy figure, devoted, submissive, and wise enough to "know her place."

In this story, a young widow (Claudette Colbert) with a young daughter hires an amiable maid, also with a small daughter. Inspired by the delicious pancakes of the maid, Aunt Delilah (Louise Beavers), Mrs. Pullman decides to open a flapjack stand on the boardwalk. She does so, and it is such a great success that within a few years she is marketing the pancake flour commercially and her future is made.

The subplot develops around the unhappiness of Delilah's daughter (Fredi Washington), whose attempts to mix socially with whites are always frustrated when her dark-skinned mother appears. Finally she runs away from home to pass for white. Only after her mother has died of a broken heart does she return.

Black journalists were joined by white film critics in denouncing the film for its handling of racial issues. On December 8, 1934, an article in *Literary Digest* stated,

(B)

The real story is merely hinted at, never really

contemplated; it is that of the beautiful, rebellious daughter of the loyal black friend. She is light-skinned, sensitive, tempestuous, and grows bitterly indignant when she sees that the white girl with whom she was reared is getting all the fine things in life, while she is subjected to humiliation and defeat.

Actually she is the most important and interesting person in the theme of the book and the picture. Her tragedy is most poignant, but the producers not only confined her to a minor and carefully handled sub-plot, but also showed their distaste for her. While her mother is treated with sympathy and warmth because she is the submissive, old-fashioned Negro who, as the saying goes, "knows her place," the daughter is too bitter and lacking in resignation over her undeserved fate.

Fredi Washington and Louise Beavers became caught in the middle of a journalistic controversy between Fannie Hurst, the author of the book on which the film was based, and Sterling Brown, a professor of the history of the theater at Howard University and film critic for the magazine *Opportunity.* Brown charged that the characters of the two women were outrageously slanted, while Hurst claimed that she had portrayed them with "integrity and accuracy."

However, many reviewers, white as well as black, agreed with Brown when he said that the rebellious daughter, in her attempt to pass for white because she could not endure the mistreatment she suffered as a Negro, showed more self-respect than the mother, whose mealymouthed servility was typical of the devoted black mammy. In criticizing the film, Brown referred to the scene in which Louise Beavers tells Claudette Colbert that she wants no share of the profits of their jointly owned pancake venture, which owed its origin to Aunt Delilah's organizational ability. She prefers to remain with Colbert in a semiservile capacity, justifying her attitude with pious phrases about keeping one's place and accepting one's lot in life.

To Brown, this attitude was ludicrous and unjust, but Hurst was extremely hurt at the criticisms. Committing an indiscretion that others would repeat throughout the thirties, she expressed the opinion that Negroes should be grateful to her for discussing black problems in her work. Black journalists were to call the advocates of this attitude "the white supremacists of the arts."

As a result of her role in *Imitation of Life,* Fredi Washington received many letters from black fellow actors congratulating her for the bite and dynamism she brought to her part despite the writing and direction. She left Hollywood soon thereafter for the Negro

Federal Theater in Washington, D.C., to spend the remainder of her career in a theater that welcomed her militancy, rare as it was for 1934. She reportedly told friends that she was not sorry to have sacrificed screen prominence for her ideals. She said she never would perpetuate outrageous stereotypes just to sustain the illusions of some "poor white trash—rich white trash too."

The film's publicity agents, on the other hand, published a self-congratulatory press release concerning *Imitation of Life.*

> Sociological experiments are by no means the purpose of filmmaking, and the few daring souls who have invaded this most controversial of all fields have met with disastrous failures. Yet there is a tendency in 1935 to depart somewhat from the standardized forms of screen literature and to liberalize this medium to conform with modern tolerance and thought. . . . There has been a marked decrease in that form of intolerance which specializes in drawing color lines, and your colored performer of merit now shares marquee distinction with the whites.

In 1935, Hollywood cynicism was carried to an extreme in *So Red the Rose* with Margaret Sullavan, Randolph Scott, and black actors Daniel Haynes and Clarence Muse. This story, directed by King Vidor, is another Civil War story, this time showing the decline and fall of a one-proud Louisiana family. The war is kept in the background, for the real war, for Vidor, takes place on the plantation.

As the men go off to war, Margaret Sullavan is left to hold the fort in the crumbling mansion. The slaves rebel, and here Haynes and Muse are pitted against each other, with Muse playing a black demagogue and Haynes the Uncle Tom dupe. Margaret Sullavan, presenting the case for Southern chivalry, "white supremacy, kindness, and courage," makes an absurd appeal to the rebellious slaves, savage brutes that they are, to calm down and stay at their posts. This was probably the most racist film of the thirties. As a result, Daniel Haynes, like Fredi Washington, left Hollywood, bitter at having agreed to take a role that had contributed to race hatred.

The thirties saw a beginning of articulate black consciousness. The American Negro Theater was born as an offshoot of the Federal Theater, which was a Government-sponsored theater formed to help the many actors and actresses unemployed because of the Depression. Here, free of the prejudice inherent in the

Daniel L. Haynes with Walter Connolly and Janet Beecher in the same film.

Daniel L. Haynes threatens Clarence Muse in *So Red the Rose* (1935).

Scenes from
The Emperor Jones
(1933)

Paul Robeson.

Paul Robeson.

Hollywood system, actors, writers, and technicians worked together to produce excellent plays at reasonable prices. Director Hallie Flanagan said of the theater,

> We live in a changing world. . . . The movies, in their kaleidoscopic speed of juxtaposition of external objects and internal emotions, are seeking to find visible and audible expression for the tempo and psychology of our time. The stage too must experiment—with ideas, with psychological relationships of men and women, with speech and rhythm forms, with dance and movement, with color and light—or it must and should become a museum product.

In the theater, *Show Boat*, soon to be made into a film, had helped abolish taboos on blacks, and theater landmarks had been established for Negro performers in *Porgy*, *Porgy and Bess*, and *The Green Pastures*. However, many black performers found it necessary to go abroad to work. Singer, dancer, actress Josephine

A nightclub scene with Harold Nicholas.

With Dudley Digges.

Baker, who had begun her career as a chorus girl in the 1920s, was one of these. By 1951 she had a nondiscrimination clause in all her contracts. Paul Robeson spent 1936 to 1939 filming in England. He voiced a complaint that, had he made it a few years before, would have cost him his career, but it was one that many black actors and actresses could share. "My reputation as a singer has misled producers into bypassing my reputation as an actor. Film producers take the attitude that the Negro must be a romantic puppet or else be of no interest to filmgoers at all."

It was a measure of black Hollywood's progress that within a few years of the appearance of *The Emperor Jones,* Robeson had become the most sought-after black actor in the world. He was also on his way to national prominence as a race hero.

The Emperor Jones was the first vehicle for a black star whose supporting players were white. It was also a revolutionary film—so revolutionary that it was a financial failure. Its limited distribution and lack of financial success retired its two young producers, John Krimsky and Gifford Cochran, from filmmaking. Based closely on Eugene O'Neill's play, the action of *The Emperor Jones* is a departure from the ordinary. Except for the realistic opening and closing scenes, it is an excursion into the mind of Brutus Jones (Robeson), a man who in ten years on "de Pullman's ca's listenin' to de white quality talk" learned a lesson: "For de big stealin' dey makes you emperor and puts you in de Hall o' Fame when you croaks."

In the playbill of the Provincetown Playhouse's production of *The Spook Sonata* in 1924, O'Neill wrote, referring to *The Emperor Jones,* "We have taken too many snap-shots of each other in every graceless position: we have endured too much from the banality of surfaces."

In the film, Jones climbs steadily from Pullman porter to emperor of the small island whose monarch he has deposed. He gains power through committing many crimes. He finally meets retribution, hunted in the jungle. The most significant aspect is that his plunge into the jungle makes the transition to a new level of reality. From this point forward, the visions and the drumbeat intensify as the film's events retreat into Jones's mind and Jones retreats into his past until he can go no further.

His is a flight into self-discovery and also an attempt to elude the self. His escape is not really from the natives of his island or from the world, but from knowledge of his own guilt. But just as his physical flight leads him in a circle back to his pursuers, his mental flight leads him back to his past, driven by a

Scenes from
The Green Pastures
(1935)

(A)

(C)

(A) Oscar Polk (The Angel Gabriel) with Rex Ingram (De Lawd) in *The Green Pastures* (1936). (B) Myrtle Anderson and Rex Ingram as Adam and Eve. (C) Eddie Anderson and Rex Ingram.

fear that acts as a catalyst to release his true self, the identity beneath the emperor's mask.

The Emperor Jones, as both a play and a film, was a major attempt to capture the essence of the American black experience. It dealt with the tribulations that everyday experience imposed on blacks.

As drama critic Doris Falk indicated, O'Neill was dealing, in *The Emperor Jones,* with Jung's concept of the collective unconscious.

> The mind of a given man contains ideas from the collective unconscious which came to him simply by virtue of his membership in the human race, as well as ideas inherited from his own specific race, tribe and family. His mind contains, in addition, unconscious ideas and symbols arising from his unique personal situation to make up the structure of his personal unconscious. Finally, from this personal unconscious emerges his own consciousness, his ego.

Jones's journey is a retrogression into his own unconsciousness and then into the collective unconsciousness of his race.

Critic Alan Overmyer says that this reversion is also Nietzschean. The atavistic theme is like one of Nietzche's aphorisms in which he defines man as one who, "in outbursts of passions and the delusions of dreams and madness, rediscovers his own primitive history, and that of humanity: animality and its savage grimaces."

Reviews across the country were generally favorable, despite the film's limited distribution. There was, however, some adverse criticism. Robert Stebbins saw white chauvinism at work in the depiction of Jones as a bragging criminal exploiting members of his own race. Some critics emphasized that the superstitious fear that brought about his disgrace and finally his death was another product of white views of blacks. But Robert F. Whitman, in *O'Neill's Search for a Language of the Theatre,* placed these aspects within the essential conflict of the play, the source of the film. *The Emperor Jones* is Robeson's best-known film and established his career and his special role in Hollywood as a living myth.

A less impressive film, but one that deserves a special place in the revolution of black Hollywood as well as of serious filmmaking, was a 1937 Warner Bros. production, *They Won't Forget.* Directed by Mervyn LeRoy, whose reputation had been established by *Little Caesar* (1931), starring Edward G. Robinson, *They Won't Forget* was a tough-minded condemnation of lynch law and gave Claude Rains his

best role to date. The film also featured Allyn Joslyn, Gloria Dickson, Edward Norris and Clinton Rosemond.

They Won't Forget is adapted from Ward Greene's novel *Death in the Deep South* and set in a small Southern town where the prosecutor, Andy Griffin (Claude Rains), is waiting for an opportunity to enhance his chances of being elected to the senate. His chance comes when the daughter of a prominent citizen is murdered. There are four suspects—the highly respected Colonel Buxton, a mill hand, a schoolteacher from the North, and the black janitor who found the body.

The prosecutor selects the murderer according to political expediency. Tump, the janitor, is a nigger; therefore, he is not a good suspect politically. If either the colonel or the mill hand were found guilty, a sector of the society would become politically alienated. The most suitable suspect, then, is the outsider from the

Clinton Rosemond in *They Won't Forget* (1937).

North, and accordingly "the trial of the century" is conducted and the teacher is duly hanged for the crime. The innocent Tump is blackjacked to ensure that he keeps on knowing his place.

Aside from *Fury* (1936), which was all-white, this was the first antilynching film, with blacks in the cast opposing lynching. *They Won't Forget* is important, too, in that it broke the traditional pattern of antiblack films set in the Deep South. The film centered both on the treatment of blacks in the South and on the distorted values of whites. Basil Wright, reviewing the film for *World Film News,* called it

> . . . a savage, horrifying, cynical and unequivocable expose of the backwardness and degeneration of the small towns in the Southern states, which have their lynchings and their Scottsboro trials, make American justice stink to high heaven.

Frank Nugent, in *The New York Times,* said that the film

> with courage, objectivity and simple eloquence, creates a brilliant sociological drama and a trenchant film editorial against intolerance and hatred.

Rosemond with E. Alyn Warren and Clifford Soubier.

Also in 1937, *Black Legion,* in which the Ku Klux Klan made an appearance, was released. Humphrey Bogart, Ann Sheridan, and Alonzo Price starred in this film, in which an attempt seemed to be made to justify the Klan's oppression of Negroes. However, this movie was so weak that only Bogart's appearance saved it from total failure.

Another film with a Southern theme, though on a different level, was *Huckleberry Finn* (1939), in which Mickey Rooney played Huck to Rex Ingram's Jim. Like many another Hollywood film with a Southern theme, *Huckleberry Finn* was made twice more in the next twenty years. In later years, the black-white togetherness this film featured would reappear in films like *The Learning Tree, The Defiant Ones,* and other escape-from-the law movies.

In the thirties, Black stars began to come into their own as artists, even though most of their roles were still stereotyped. Not until the last few years of the decade, however, did popular films like *Gone with the Wind* (1939) and *Kentucky* (1938) give certain blacks a prominent place in the Hollywood community. Only now did actors like Eddie "Rochester" Anderson, Rex Ingram, Hattie McDaniel, and Paul Robeson become recognized as stars. However, although Hattie McDaniel, for instance, made twenty films in the thirties, Robeson made his reputation on a mere handful, of which his last, *Show Boat* (1936), put him in the kind of "singing nigger" role of which he later complained.

This was the second film version of *Show Boat.* In the first, made in 1929, Harry Pollard, the director of

Hattie McDaniel holding Buckwheat in *Anniversary Trouble* (1935). With Claudia Dell, Johnny Arthur and Spanky McFarland.

the 1927 version of *Uncle Tom's Cabin,* directed a heavily melodramatic structure. Several recorded songs from the Jerome Kern score were played as a prologue to this story of a gambling showboat, ambling its way down the Mississippi, and the lives it affects. The changing fortunes of Laura La Plante's Magnolia and her attempt to reform her drinking husband, Gaylord (Joseph Schildkraut), provide the main story of the film. Gaylord's fall is symbolized by a picture of checks going up in flame over a roulette wheel; he buys a horse and it loses because of foul play at the track; he gets drunk. The film's closing scenes are less melodramatic, with the song "Ol' Man River" bringing the melodrama to an end.

The 1936 version of the film, with Paul Robeson, Hattie McDaniel, Irene Dunne, and Allan Jones, differed very little from the previous version. Robeson's voice and a certain polish and softness were the only notable additions.

Neither *Show Boat* nor *Gone with the Wind* made any changes in the Hollywood treatment of blacks. However, Hattie McDaniel won an Academy Award as best supporting actress for her portrayal of the role of the mammy in *Gone with the Wind,* becoming the first Negro ever to win the prize. Of this role, Miss McDaniel said in an early interview, "The only choice permitted us is either to be servants for $7.00 a week or portray them for $700.00 a week." Best known for her servant roles, she later reiterated that it was "much better to play a maid than to be one."

Some black critics felt that Hattie McDaniel's superior acting ability transcended the part she played over and over again. Others thought that she should have used her popularity as a lever to obtain better parts. Asked on numerous occasions why she did not aspire to larger, more diversified parts, she would answer that she would rather be at the top of what she knew best.

Another reason for her reluctance to widen her acting spectrum is reflected in a statement made by Lena Horne, who also began her career as a singer.

> I always wanted to be an actress ever since I traveled with my mother in the Lafayette Stock Company. But it is easier for a colored person to be a singer than an actress; one's color is to be reckoned with in every field. A singer is accepted when an actress is not.

Another typecast black actress, Butterfly McQueen, appeared in *Gone with the Wind* as a moronic servant girl. *Gone with the Wind* was her first film. Later, in *Cabin in the Sky* and *Mildred Pierce,* she would play basically the same role. In her last film, *Duel in the Sun* (1947), she broke that tradition.

Black participation in *Gone with the Wind* was peripheral to the main attraction, the love story of Rhett (Clark Gable) and Scarlett O'Hara (Vivien Leigh). David O. Selznick had waited to start filming until he had the stars he wanted. For the first time in a film with this theme, producers and directors paid close attention to detail, wanting to make the background as authentic as possible. The NAACP could also congratulate itself for having persuaded the director to change some lines that cast slurs upon blacks. For example, Scarlett's reference to "free niggers" was changed to "freedmen."

The thirties movies began to change the image of the Negro in film. Black performers, especially singers and dancers, began to rise professionally, and the white press joined the black press in demanding greater equality and an end to racist themes in film. Hollywood did not fully use the talents of its black performers, but nonetheless, the black star was emerging. Hattie McDaniel's award, Butterfly McQueen's rise to prominence, Rex Ingram's popularity, Paul Robeson's classic performance in *The Emperor Jones,* and many other excellent and popular Negro performances all contributed enormously to the rise of black Hollywood.

Eddie Anderson

(A) Eddie Anderson with Theresa Harris in *Buck Benny Rides Again* (1939). (B) Anderson with Fields in *You Can't Cheat an Honest Man* (1939). (c) *Jezebel* (1938).

(A)

(B)

(c)

Paul Robeson.

Paul Robeson, Irene Dunne, Hattie McDaniel, Helen Morgan.

Hattie McDaniel, Paul Robeson.

(Right) Sammy White, Charles Winninger, Irene Dunne, Hattie McDaniel, Allan Jones, Paul Robeson.

Scenes from
Gone With the Wind
(1939)

(A)   (B)

(A) Ben Carter is between Fred Crane and
George Reeves. (B) Butterfly McQueen and
Vivien Leigh. (C) Oscar Polk with Vivien
Leigh. (D) Hattie McDaniel and Olivia
De Havilland. (E) Eddie Anderson, the
faithful family retainer. (F) Miss McDaniel
with Clark Gable.

(C)

(D)

(E)

(F)

(B)

(C)

(D)

(A)

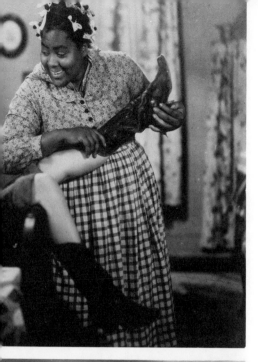

Louise Beavers

(E)

(A) Louise Beavers and Kay Francis in
Girls About Town (1931). (B) With
Joan Bennett in *Wild Girl* (1932).
(C) With Joan Crawford, Mary Doran
in *Our Blushing Brides* (1930). (D) With
Helen Jerome Eddy and Claudette Colbert
in *Manslaughter* (1932). (E) With James
Stewart in *No Time For Comedy* (1940).

Spanky and Cotton. (1935)

Theresa Harris

Theresa Harris, Clark Gable and George Reed in *Hold Your Man* (1933).

Frank Darien, Theresa Harris, Franklin Pangborn, Frank McHugh and Gregory Ratoff in *Professional Sweetheart* (1933).

The Nicholas Brothers

(B)

(A) *Jealousy* (1934). (B) Harold Nicholas
with George Murphy and Eddie Cantor in
Kid Millions (1934). (C) *Tin Pan Alley*
(1940). (D) With George Burns in
The Big Broadcast of 1936.

Clarence Muse

Clarence Muse, Jackie Cooper, and Wallace Beery in *O'Shaughnessy's Boy* (1935).

A scene from Frank Capra's *Broadway Bill* (1934). Clarence Muse with Charles Middleton, Warner Baxter and Myrna Loy.

Joe Louis plays himself in *Spirit of Youth* (1938). Clarence Muse and Mantan Moreland are on his right.

Clarence Muse shares a scene in *The Mind Reader* (1933) with Allen Jenkins, Constance Cummings and Warren William.

(A) Ann Shoemaker, Fred MacMurray
Hattie McDaniel, Katharine Hepburn,
Fred Stone in *Alice Adams* (1935).
(B) Two scenes from *Judge Priest* (1935).

Hattie McDaniel

A portfolio of scenes from the 1930's

(A)

(B)

(A) Stymie Beard. (B) Buckwheat with
Darla Hood in *Our Gang Follies of 1938*.
(C) Fredi Washington. (D) Paul Muni and
Everett Brown in *I Am a Fugitive From
a Chain Gang* (1932). (E) Etta Moten
singing "The Carioca" in *Flying Down
to Rio* (1933).

(A) Cab Calloway in the first *Big Broadcast* (1932). (B) Jennie LeGon and Bill
Robinson in *Hooray for Love* (1935). (C) Cab Calloway leads the chorus in *The
Singing Kid* (1936). (D) Dick Powell and the Mills Brothers in *Happiness Ahead*
(1934). (E) Louis Armstrong trumpets for Martha Raye in *Artists and Models*
(1937).

(D)

(E)

(A)

(B)

(C)

(D)

Mae West and Marlene Dietrich and their maids

(A) Gertrude Howard in *I'm No Angel*
(1933). (B) Louise Beavers in *She Done
Him Wrong* (1933). (C) Libby Taylor in
Belle of the Nineties (1934). (D) Lillian
Yarbo in *Destry Rides Again* (1939).

The Black Independents in the 1930's

(A)

(A) Oscar Polk and Bea Freeman in *Underworld* (1936). (B) (C) From *God's Stepchildren* (1938). (Right) Lurid pressbook cover for *Temptation* (1936). (Overleaf) Scenes from *Temptation*

(B)

STICK CHESTER

BEE FREEMAN

SEYMORE

ETHEL MOSES

SEYMORE

DEZ ROGERS

"TEMPTATION"

The episode of the "Mad Mullah" running alternately through the story, gives the picture splendid musical relief. Starred in the Cabaret sequences are the popular Pope Sisters, Bobby Hargreaves snappy Kit Kat Club Orchestra, Lillian Fitzgerald, Raymond Kallund, "roping fool," Dot and Dash, tap Dancers, the "Six Sizzlers," performing orchestra, (two bands) Taft Rice, entertainer, and other acts and musical numbers.

(A) *Gang War* (1940) starred Ralph
Cooper (center), with Gladys Snyder
(Left) and Jess Lee Brooks (Right)
(B) Another scene from *Gang War*.
(C) Poster for *Son of Ingagi* (1937).
(D) A saloon scene from *The Bronze
Buckaroo* (1939), a popular black Western
which starred Herb Jeffries, standing at the
bar with guns drawn.

(c)

(d)

103

(A)

(B)

(A) Spencer Williams, Jr., and
Connie Harris. (B) Herb Jeffries.
(C) Mantan Moreland (tied to tree)
Spencer Williams, Jr., and Herb Jeffries.

(A)

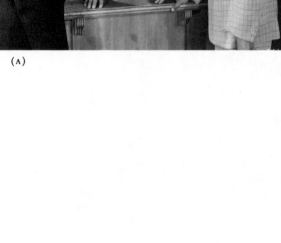

Scenes from
Dark Manhattan
(1937)

(A) Clinton Rosemond (center) and
Ralph Cooper (right), (B) Ralph
Cooper and Cleo Herndon

(B)

Chapter 4
The Forties

Despite the upheaval of World War II, despite the promises of the New Deal, the forties were an era of slow, almost infinitesimal change in the area of civil rights.

Although an end to the struggle for equal opportunity seemed distant, black people were better off financially. Roosevelt abolished the segregation of federal offices in Washington and used the power of his office to bring integration to the armed forces and to the work programs set up under the New Deal. The president appointed scores of blacks to public office, including officials like Harold Ickes, Secretary of the Interior, and he sought the voices of blacks in almost every new bureau and commission. As a result of his and Mrs. Roosevelt's efforts, in 1946 there were four times as many black federal employees as there had been in 1933.

In professional sports, Jackie Robinson broke the color line and opened up a major profession that had formerly been a "closed shop."

The film industry, however, continued to reflect the more backward social attitudes. When the decade opened, musicals featuring both black and white performers were completely segregated. Individual scenes had to be either all-white or all-black. This created some rather bizarre situations. For instance, the black members of Benny Goodman's combo were segregated from the white musicians and were never featured as soloists. In the band's film appearances it was never apparent that Lionel Hampton and Charley Christian were the driving forces of the group. They were seen vaguely hovering in the background, and before the films could be sent to the South, distributors were required to delete any scenes that suggested that the band was integrated.

The films of black Hollywood in the forties were of two main types—all-black or mostly black movies and white movies in which one or more blacks appeared, usually for light relief. It is significant that many black actors in the second category left lasting impressions on audiences despite their often mediocre roles. Although most black roles still represented the old Hollywood stereotypes, individual black performers were sometimes able to transcend their roles, to lend them additional character and make them memorable.

Hattie McDaniel continued unspectacularly

throughout the forties as the archetypal Aunt Jemima to various Hollywood beauties and families of Southern aristocracy. Eddie "Rochester" Anderson, who had arrived at the end of the thirties as Jack Benny's pop-eyed foil, continued to make movies throughout the forties, usually playing the same type of character his appearances with Benny had led audiences to expect.

Another black actor who was constantly employed during this period was Mantan Moreland. Inspired by the successes of the Benny-Anderson team, in 1940 Monogram Pictures initiated a series featuring Moreland with Frankie Darro. The series, directed by Howard Bretherton, began with *Chasing Trouble,* followed by *Farewell to Fame, In the Night, Up in the Air,* and *You're Out of Luck.* In this series of lively escapist films, not unlike some of today's action adventures, the pair solved mysteries, foiled robbery attempts, brought criminals to justice, and demonstrated the importance of being on the right side of the law. The series featured only action and made no attempt at social meaning.

Darro had also appeared in many thirties films in which he had portrayed the tough kid with a heart of gold. He was very popular with black audiences, who admired his bravado and his ability to take care of any situation. His films with Moreland were the earliest forerunners of the seventies' audience-identification films displaying superheavy heros such as *Shaft* and *Super Fly.*

Moreland, who portrayed a character very much in the Stepin Fetchit tradition, had become so popular by the end of the series that he was immediately transferred to the Charlie Chan series. This proved to be his undoing as an actor, for after he had played Charlie Chan's bug-eyed stooge for several years, his identity as a buffoon was so firmly established that he was inescapably typecast. In films such as *Charlie Chan in Black Magic, The Scarlet Clue, Shanghai Cobra, The Red Dragon, Dark Alibi, The Jade Mask,* and *Cabin in the Sky,* Moreland displayed himself as the classic foolish, servile clown. It is unfortunate that Moreland is remembered only as a servant and a clown, for he was an excellent character actor, as he showed in *Bowery to Broadway,* in which, ironically enough, he brilliantly captured the underlying pathos in the life of a vaudeville comedian. Moreland's professional career resembled those of many other black Hollywood actors in that he had to compromise to survive.

Other black actors of this period refused to accept roles they considered insulting to their people. For most of these few, notably Butterfly McQueen and Leigh Whipper, this was professional suicide. Others like Lena Horne and Paul Robeson, and for some time Leigh Whipper, were able to refuse parts they considered racist and survive as performers. Unfortunately, the courageous behavior of those actors and actresses who did take a stand did little to stem the tide of insulting but financially profitable films.

Butterfly McQueen played her last servant-girl role in 1945 in *Mildred Pierce,* with Joan Crawford. After this she said that she would never again play a scatterbrained maid or a superstitious comic servant. Like Fredi Washington before her, she left her film career behind. She had played her particular stereotype too well, and producers were not prepared to offer her anything else. True to her word, she never appeared in her old image again; in later years, when she was approached with an offer to re-create it, she refused.

One way for black actors and actresses to survive without compromising their beliefs might have been to work for independent black producers, of whom there were a small number during the forties. Unfortunately, black producers did not necessarily make films of any more social relevance than their white colleagues.

One black producer, Ted Toddy, serves as an example. Many obstacles faced a neophyte black capitalist of the time—problems that would have been encountered by anyone with a strong social conscience, which Toddy by no means had. To raise capital for a black enterprise and to keep producing, he needed an immediate return on his investment, and this resulted in his making slipshod films on short shooting schedules. Learning from the methods of Oscar Micheaux, he improvised enough to make some mediocre films on a shoestring budget. His opinions about what the Negro public wanted did not involve him in any crises of conscience. He wrote in *Motion Picture Herald,*

> Negro audiences do not care for the heavily emotional dramas. Their choice in film entertainment is the picture which features light comedy, outdoor adventures, or musical comedies with an abundance of singing and dancing and comedy-romance.

This statement sounds more like a routine plea for financing than an analysis of the place of the black film. Toddy was lacking in social perception, for he made the above statement in 1947, the year of Jackie Robinson's appearance with the Brooklyn Dodgers and the first publication of Ralph Ellison's *The Invisible Man.*

Toddy Pictures produced their first all-black movie, *Bronze Venus,* in 1940. The thin plot detailed

Mantan Moreland

With Roland Winters as Charlie Chan in *Mystery of the Golden Eye* (1948).

The Chinese Ring (1947).

the lurid adventures of a musical celebrity, portrayed by Lena Horne, but for whom the film would have been a total failure. Her electrifying performance gave the film what success it had. Also starring in *Bronze Venus* was leading man Ralph Cooper.

Toddy's other films, all in a similar vein of escapist-romantic entertainment and mostly using somewhat hackneyed material, included *Mantan Dresses Up.*

To be fair to Toddy, he could hardly, as so marginal an operator, afford to take risks that even successful, big-time producers were not prepared to take. Prejudice worked against the black producer in various ways, not the least of which was the closed shop existing in the technical trade unions. The black producer was faced with the difficulty of finding competent Negro light, sound, and camera technicians. Editors, screenwriters, cutters, and directors were equally rare. Blacks had no access to training and little or no opportunity to develop technical skills. Other problems lay in the difficulty of purchasing film equipment because of the lack of credit for blacks. So a host of race-related issues made the problems of a black producer almost insurmountable even before the question of film content was considered.

But even if he had lived in another era, in which prejudice was less blatant and the expression of black culture and experience considered valid, Ted Toddy would probably not have produced great films. An apt comment on the films he and many of his colleagues were making is contained in the following criticism, published in *Sight and Sound* in 1939.

> The conclusion is inescapable that independent Negro producers have lacked the social vision needed if the Negro is to be represented truly and fully in the cinema today, and if the stereotypes in which he is cast are to be discarded. The dramatic possibilities of Negro life, which are so rich and varied, and the potential of the Negro actor, already demonstrated in the poor media accessible to him now, will reveal themselves fully when this social vision arrives.

Hollywood's own "black" movies followed the pattern established in the previous decade. The blacks were happy-go-lucky clowns with rhythm. Rhythm is very important in the forties movies. Paramount centered *Birth of the Blues* (1941) around Jack Teagarden's orchestra and hot jazz renditions of "Memphis Blues," "St. Louis Blues," and "Melancholy Baby." The orchestra's frenetic jamming enlivens the flirtation between Bing Crosby and Mary Martin. Eddie

(Rochester) Anderson also appears in this film, which was directed by Victor Schertzinger. Of all the films about jazz made in this period, *Birth of the Blues* is the most faithful.

William Dieterle, on the other hand, proved in his film *Syncopation* (1942) that he knew next to nothing about jazz and even less about black musicians. His image of the American Negro seems to have been derived from a summer rerun of *Show Boat,* which, in a film intended to show the evolution of jazz, is not a very helpful starting point. In the film, Jackie Cooper plays a tormented jazz musician going from club to club with his "baby," Bonita Granville. Readings from the poetry of Walt Whitman are thrown in. There is little of the "syncopation" of the title.

According to Hollywood, all Negroes belonged down South singing hymns and keeping out of trouble. In Darryl Zanuck's *Maryland* (1940) Ben Carter as Shadrach gets religion at a Negro revival meeting. This scene, in which Clarence Muse officiates as the good minister, is played with a fair amount of sensitivity. The characters in *Maryland* are the usual stereotypes, however, and include a gregarious maid played by Hattie McDaniel.

Much the same clichés about black life appear in *Cabin in the Sky,* the 1943 film based on the successful Broadway musical of the same name. Many black critics condemned its racial attitudes, but as the first all-black movie musical in many years, it was a major achievement in both form and content. Director Vincente Minnelli expanded the stage musical into what many critics have felt was the best black movie musical ever made. It fused a strong book with delightful music, including songs like "Taking a Chance on Love," "Happiness Is Just a Thing Called Joe," and "Life's Full of Consequences."

The story of *Cabin in the Sky* concerns a battle for the soul of Little Joe Jackson (Eddie Anderson). Unbeknown to him or his wife (Ethel Waters), a classic battle is being waged for him. On one side is Lucifer, Jr., played by Rex Ingram, with the boys from Hades; on the other, are the soldiers of heaven, who are attempting with Ethel Waters's help, to keep Joe on the straight and narrow path during the six-month reprieve from death he has been given. It is a formidable task to prevent Joe from falling into Lucifer's traps, the most tempting of which is seductress Georgia Brown, played by Lena Horne.

Lena Horne's first Hollywood film had been *Panama Hattie* (1942), in which she made a brief appearance but made a tremendous impact with her remarkable voice. She also appeared in Fox's all-black

(B)

(A) John Bubbles and Ethel Waters.
(B) Lena Horne and Eddie
Anderson. (C) Ethel Waters,
Butterfly McQueen, Kenneth
Spencer and Clinton Rosemond.

(C)

(D)

(E)

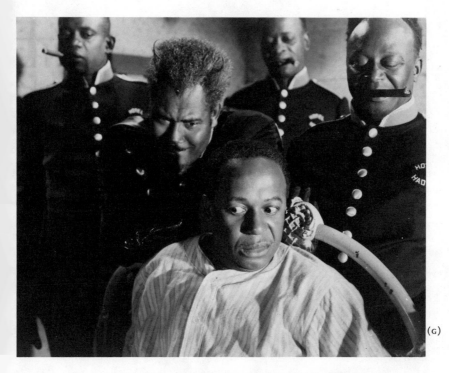

(G)

(D) Miss Lena Horne. (E) Miss Waters
and Eddie Anderson. (F) Louis Armstrong,
Rex Ingram and Mantan Moreland.
(G) Eddie Anderson menaced by Rex
Ingram and Mantan Moreland (far right).

Lena Horne singing the title song.

The Nicholas Brothers.

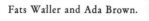

116

Fats Waller and Ada Brown.

Lena Horne and Bill Robinson.

Cab Calloway doing "The Jumpin' Jive."

Bill Robinson and Lena Horne.

Scenes from
Stormy Weather
(1943)

Lena Horne

Broadway Rhythm (1941): "The Brazilian Boogie-Woogie."

musical offering *Stormy Weather*. This film, which fell far short of the magnificence of *Cabin in the Sky* and was made in the same year, is more a revue than a musical with a plot. It is primarily a showcase for the talents of Lena Horne and Bill Robinson, and its plot consists of a series of vignettes about this pair of screen lovers.

Lena Horne's success story is striking and heartening. As a singer, she went within a few years from a chorus job in Harlem's Cotton Club to co-starring with Adelaide Hall, Cab Calloway, and the Nicholas Brothers. She became a lead singer in Noble Sissle's band, and then with Charlie Barnet's orchestra she became the first black female vocalist to be featured with a white dance band. A year later, she was appearing in the Mocambo Club in Hollywood, where MGM discovered her and offered her the role in *Panama Hattie*. Her later films included *Ziegfeld Follies, Two Girls and a Sailor, Thousands Cheer,* and many others.

At this time Negro performers were refused official unionization in Hollywood. The way casting was usually done was that a white producer would call up a Negro actor, who would set himself up as a surrogate agent. The agent would be rewarded with one of the better parts of the film.

To combat this and other injustices, a handful of black performers organized themselves into a quasi-union. It became almost impossible for a black actor or actress to get work without the recommendation of this group, who protested loudly when anything threatened their control. They ostracized Lena Horne when she got a role directly from the producer of *Cabin in the Sky*. The group claimed that she was ruining the chances of other black actresses.

Actually, Lena Horne was a campaigner for fair treatment of black performers. As a board member of the Screen Actors Guild she has represented black film actors for nearly thirty years. She was one of the first black performers to be able to survive in Hollywood as a star despite refusing roles she considered demeaning to her race.

Leigh Whipper also refused stereotyped roles. Originally a stage actor, he had appeared in Broadway in *Talk of the Town, The Squaw Man, Trial of Mary Dugan,* and *Porgy.* Two early-forties films, *Of Mice and Men* and *The Ox-Bow Incident,* established him as an intelligent performer who would not play parts that made the Negro into a figure of derision.

In the United Artists version of the John Steinbeck

Ziegfeld Follies (1946): "Love."

novel *Of Mice and Men,* Whipper played Crook, the character who provides the philosophical commentary to the story. *Of Mice and Men* starred Lon Chaney as Lennie, a gentle giant whose mind is not clear "on accounta he'd been kicked in the head by a horse." Not knowing his own strength, the mentally retarded Lenny one day kills Mae, the wife of the foreman of the work gang of which he and his partner, George, are members. Knowing that Lenny is sure to be lynched, George must kill his friend, and this he does while telling Lenny about the time when they will have their own little place.

The Ox-Bow Incident, very different from the powerfully compassionate *Of Mice and Men,* also involves a lynch mob. An emotional story of a posse that hangs the wrong men for murder, it was made three years after *Of Mice and Men,* in 1943. Whipper played a Negro preacher who, in one of the most poignant scenes, pleads with the angry mob for the lives of the accused men. Peter Noble describes this scene in *The Negro in Film.*

(Above) Leigh Whipper and Henry Fonda in *The Ox-Bow Incident* (1943).

(Top) Lon Chaney, Jr., Roman Bohnan and Leigh Whipper in *Of Mice and Men* (1939).

> As he declares, he comes from a race which has had to bear the brunt of lynch law, and lynching is no way to settle things for black or white people.

George Brent, Ernest Anderson and Bette Davis in a scene from *In This Our Life* (1942).

None of Whipper's other films, which included *Virginia* (1941), *White Cargo* (1942), *Untamed Fury* (1947), and *Lost Boundaries* (1949), were of quite the same caliber as his two best-known films. However, all his roles had a dignity unusual for black parts. In some cases, when a script bothered him, he would make arrangements with the director to cut offending passages. Still, most of the parts he played, however true to life, were of farmhands and servants. Not until the fifties would the educated black begin making an appearance, with Sidney Poitier.

There was one exception. In the film *In This Our Life* (1942), Bette Davis blames a hit and run murder, of which she is guilty, on a black man. Not only is the black educated, but as Bosley Crowther wrote in *The New York Times,* in an otherwise poor film . . .

the one successful component of the film . . . [is] this brief but frank allusion to racial discrimination. And it is presented in a realistic manner, uncommon to Hollywood, by the definition of the Negro as an educated and comprehending character.

The dignified young black law student who maintained his innocence was played by Ernest Anderson.

World War II would bring many changes, but in the film industry, it would take some time for evolving social attitudes to come through. In *Blacks in American Films: Today and Yesterday,* Edward Mapp makes the point that most war films excluded blacks, and where Negroes did appear there were never more than one or two. Hollywood made it clear that the war was won by white America. Three films Mapp used to illustrate his point are *Crash Dive* (1943), with Ben Carter as the token black, *Sahara* (1943), with Rex Ingram as Tambul, and *Bataan* (1943), with Kenneth Spencer as Wesley Epps. He goes on to quote William E. Burke's study of black actors in American films from 1946 to 1961.

In a film in which the Negro character is supposedly treated "fairly," Epps is too busy working to participate in most group scenes. When he does appear among a sizeable number of his comrades, he is distinctly relegated to the background in discussion.

MGM's *Bataan* is interesting because, quite against the intentions of the studio, the film emerged as one of the first antiwar movies to come out of Hollywood. Thirteen soldiers fight to the death as they try to bomb an obscure bridge in the middle of a worthless stretch of land. The absolute futility of this operation comes

Robert Taylor, Thomas Mitchell, Robert Walker, Kenneth Spencer and Lloyd Nolan in *Bataan* (1943).

Bogart with Rex Ingram in *Sahara* (1943).

across with great power. Kenneth Spencer's portrayal of Epps makes it clear that his strength is among the most enduring of the group. To him is given the task of saying a prayer over the jungle grave of the group's dead captain. His eloquent epitaph for the dead in all wars confirms the covert message of the film.

Zoltan Korda's *Sahara* (1943) gives the first example of a black defeating a white in fair combat. The part of the Sudanese soldier in this desert war epic is played by Rex Ingram, complete with a Southern accent. In another break from Hollywood tradition, Ingram has a servant. Korda spent a lot of time establishing the confidence the men have in the black, especially that of Humphrey Bogart, who plays the tough sergeant who leads the men into a dilapidated building where they succeed in holding off German troops.

Peter Noble was very impressed by one scene in which Ingram figured.

> He uses his hands as a cup for the drinking water which quenches the thirst of the white men. Each of the whites drinks out of the water in the hands of a Negro, and none of them finds this extraordinary.

Perhaps Noble missed the point of this scene. For one thing, the soldiers have not had water in days, and they are about to be attacked. Ingram's action is one of a black serving white men even though they are required to touch his hands to drink the water. Another point is that Ingram plays a Sudanese, not an American black, a subtle difference in attitude being the result.

Alfred Hitchcock's *Lifeboat* (1944), based on the John Steinbeck novel, also has a black, Canada Lee, a

Broadway actor turned film performer. The action takes place on a lifeboat where nine distinctly different people struggle to survive. Probably the most interesting character in the film is a Nazi survivor from the submarine that torpedoed the ship from which the other survivors escaped. The Nazi takes over steering of the lifeboat and steers it toward the open sea, rather than to the Bahamas, as everyone thought he was doing. The combination of Steinbeck and Hitchcock made this one of the most powerful dramas of the year. At one point Canada Lee, as the black steward, saves a woman passenger, and the others call him a hero. Black self-sacrifice for white people was to be a more common theme in the next decade.

American attitudes to race are reflected in *Till the End of Time* (1946), which unfortunately was not well enough made to bring its message home. This film concerns the problems three veterans have in adjusting to civilian life after the war. All have been damaged by the war—one has no legs, another has a silver plate in his head, and the third, played by Robert Mitchum, is simply very confused.

In the film many diatribes are made against injustice toward minority groups. In one scene, for example, a semifascist group called the American Patriots Association is attempting to get all ex-servicemen to petition the federal government for fair play for veterans. The leader of the group tells Mitchum that the association represents everybody except "niggers, Jews, and Catholics."

Mitchum screams back, "My best friend, a Jew, is lying back in a foxhole at Guadalcanal. I'm gonna spit in your eye for him, because we don't want to have people like you in this country."

Poor as the film was, at least Hollywood was at last acknowledging the existence of racism.

Hollywood now began to use themes that showed the American social structure more truthfully, particularly with regard to racial attitudes. Edward Mapp quotes William Loren Katz's *Eyewitness: The Negro in American History,*

> One of the biggest problems of the postwar years was that of making America a land of liberty and justice for all. Many whites had returned from Europe and Asia believing that if the idea of a "master race" was wrong for our enemies, it was wrong for America, too.

This attitude is clearly evident in a film Somerset-Screen Guild brought out in 1947, *The Burning Cross,* an exposé of the Ku Klux Klan and its successful attempts to keep blacks out of the voting booths. Though commercial banks were so fearful of white backlash that they were loath to finance this film,

The Burning Cross was more successful than anyone had anticipated. It made an honest attempt to show the conditions under which most Southern blacks lived and to plead the urgent need for a liberalization of attitudes.

However, the most successful film of the previous year was seen by the black press as one of the most potentially dangerous influences on the black image ever put out by Hollywood. This was *Song of the South* (1946), a screen adaptation of the Uncle Remus stories, made for children by Walt Disney. Children loved the film, but critics lambasted it, and black critics and the NAACP called for a boycott. It was simply unforgivable in 1947 to show a Deep South plantation as an idyllic place of sunshine and light where the contented slaves served their white master. The film featured Ruth Warrick, Hattie McDaniel as the mammy, and James Baskett as Uncle Remus, the wise old story-telling slave, a role Rex Ingram had refused. Despite some clever animation, skillful use of color, and a great deal of hackneyed Disney charm, the film was an anachronism, showing, perhaps for the last time,

Hattie McDaniel and James Baskett in *Song of the South* (1946).

Ethel Waters watching Jeanne Crain and
William Lundigan in *Pinky* (1949).

(Right) Nina Mae McKinney and Frederick
O'Neal with Jeanne Crain in *Pinky*.

James Edwards.

(Right) James Edwards offers his hand to Steve
Brodie, while Lloyd Bridges and Frank Lovejoy
look on in *Home of the Brave* (1949).

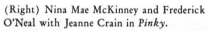

Canada Lee (right) comforts James Hilton in *Lost Boundaries* (1949).

the myth of the Old South once so dear to Hollywood. However, the fact remained that the film drew an enormous young audience into an impression against which blacks had been fighting for decades.

Another anachronistic film had appeared two years before, in 1945. *Saratoga Trunk* had Ingrid Bergman made up to look like a Creole courtesan in a film adaptation of a novel by Edna Ferber. Gary Cooper as a Texas con man and Miss Bergman take turns trying to outwit each other in an attempt to gain wealth and success. The best performance, however, was given by Flora Robson, who played Bergman's mulatto retainer.

Four films of 1949 dealt with the racial problem in different ways.

Home of the Brave showed how the war changed racial attitudes. A black soldier, Moss (James Edwards), has been fighting in the Pacific. Unable to endure white bigotry, he suffers paralysis, the point being that his condition is a psychological response to racism. His recovery is brought about by the psychiatrist screaming at him, "You dirty nigger, get up and walk!"

Two films had the theme of blacks passing for white. In 20th Century-Fox's *Pinky,* a nurse returns to her home in the South after posing as white in Boston. After a number of episodes that show Pinky going through conflicts about her masquerade, she finally gives up her false white identity along with her white boyfriend and opens up a nursing home for black children. Similarly in *Lost Boundaries* a light-skinned black physician poses as white in a New England town.

In both these films, white actors took the black roles, Jeanne Crain appearing in the title role in *Pinky.*

Will Geer and Juano Hernandez in *Intruder in the Dust* (1949).

The impact of these films was felt most profoundly by blacks who had no interest in passing for white. One recalls the very light-skinned black actress Fredi Washington and her determination to find a black role after her appearance in *Imitation of Life.* The implication in *Pinky* and *Lost Boundaries* was that all Negroes, certainly professional ones, wanted to be white, although the films tried to make the point that Pinky and the physician were forced to "pass" for purely professional reasons.

Samuel Bloom, in his study of audience reaction, stated that "when the movie's hero makes the decision to pass, it appears that the decision is forced upon him more by fellow Negroes than by whites."

The 1949 adaptation of William Faulkner's novel *Intruder in the Dust* was not only one of the best films of the year but one of the most significant films on a racial theme to come out of Hollywood.

Juano Hernandez gives a fine performance in the role of a condemned Negro waiting for the lynch mob, a man who would rather die than give up his dignity. Producer Clarence Brown brought cast and crew to Oxford, Mississippi, to film Faulkner's novel in its actual location. Brown was concerned, not so much with showing scenes of mobs and lynching—this had been done before—as with revealing the mixture of hatred and anxiety in the expressions on the faces of the people involved. The film was important in its powerful statement that for a black man in the South, there could be no justice. However, the film departed from the book in that whereas Faulkner showed the innocent man's lynching as an inevitable process because of the pride that the townsmen find insufferable in a Negro, in the film, justice is done and Lucas Beauchamp, the "intruder" of the title, is set free.

Hollywood, then, was beginning to struggle with the question of racism, even if very tentatively. Of course, the vast majority of Hollywood productions in which blacks appeared were glossy vehicles for song and dance. Between these films at one end of the spectrum and the low-budget black productions at the other, there were, in addition to a film like *Intruder in the Dust*, a rather small number of excellent documentaries on black life put out by both the studios and the independents. In 1940, the American Film Center released *One Tenth of Our Nation*. Directed by Henwar Rodakiewicz, it probed the facts about inadequate education for blacks in the South under the "separate but equal" doctrine of the Supreme Court, which prevailed until struck down by the Warren Court in 1954.

The film depicted the shortage of schools in rural areas of the South and the dilapidated conditions in existing schools. It also showed the work of the remedial program developed by the Tuskegee Institute and the efforts to spread the program into the most backward areas. Since there were no opportunities for professional or technical training for blacks, they were condemned to live as serflike sharecroppers.

Jack Goldberg produced *We've Come a Long, Long Way* in 1945 as a documentary cavalcade of the black race. Goldberg was a pioneer in black entertainment and had produced a number of all-black stage shows in New York. He also produced the first all-black newsreel and was subsequently associated with films like *Siren of the Tropics, Harlem in Heaven,* and *Mystery in Swing. We've Come a Long, Long Way* was shown in schools, colleges, and churches throughout the country.

The commercial distribution system precluded widespread screenings for such controversial films as some of the documentaries. Two particularly excellent documentaries were *As Our Boyhood Is* and *A Place to Live.* The latter was produced by the Philadelphia Housing Association to point out the patterns of racial segregation developing in Northern cities. The film graphically displayed Philadelphia's substandard housing in the old, run-down section where most blacks

Hernandez and Claude Jarman Jr. in the same film.

lived. Although the ghettos had not become as large and depressing as they are today, a middle-class white audience was shocked by the slum conditions under which blacks were forced to live.

A Place to Live might have been enormously effective had it been granted wider distribution, but few people got to see it. It was too controversial and not entertaining enough for the commercial circuits.

One documentary look at a black man's life, made by the U.S. Department of Agriculture, did get better distribution. *Henry Brown, Farmer* was directed by Roger Barlow and narrated by Canada Lee. It focused on the life of a small farmer in Alabama and was one of several movies made during the war that showed that all Americans, black and white, contributed to the war effort. The film did not try to differentiate black from white; it centered instead on Brown's farming problems.

The enthusiastic reception of *Henry Brown, Farmer* gave MGM the confidence to produce *Dr. George Washington Carver,* the finest black documentary made by the Hollywood establishment.

Clinton Rosemond played Carver, and the film presented an accurate portrayal of the man and his ideal, that all people should share in the wealth of the soil.

Carlton Moss portraying a black minister in Frank Capra's *The Negro Soldier* (1944), a U.S. Army Signal Corps film.

In the forties, black Hollywood began to expand as films tentatively explored boundaries previously untouched. Racial tension, prejudice, and injustice were to be more deeply discussed in the following decades.

(A)   (B)

Dorothy Dandridge

(A) With Count Basie in *Hit Parade of 1943*. (B) In an all-black film: *Moo Cow Boogie* (1943). (C) Singing "Chattanooga Choo Choo" with the Nicholas Brothers in *Sun Valley Serenade* (1941). (D) With Ona Munson in *Lady From Louisiana* (1941). (E) With Louis Armstrong in *Atlantic City* (1941). (F) Facing Sterling Hayden in *Bahama Passage* (1941).

(C)

(D)

(E)

(F)

(A) Eddie Anderson, Theresa Harris and Ernest Whitman in *Buck Benny Rides Again* (1940). (B) Theresa Harris confuses Eddie Anderson in *Love Thy Neighbor* (1940). (C) *Star Spangled Rhythm* (1942): Eddie Anderson and Katherine Dunham.

(A) Willie Best faces Ida Lupino and Humphrey Bogart in *High Sierra* (1941). (B) Willie Best in a *High Sierra* publicity shot. (C) Willie Best and Lon McAllister in *Home in Indiana* (1944).

131

Clinton Rosemond with Betty Field and Peter Lawford in *Flesh and Fantasy* (1943).

Rosemond with Walter Pidgeon and Greer Garson in *Blossoms in the Dust* (1941).

Louis Armstrong and Billie Holiday in *New Orleans* (1947).

Louise Beavers with Gene Tierney in *Belle Starr* (1941).

Miss Beavers and Leigh Whipper (standing) with Spring Byington in *The Vanishing Virginian* (1942).

Hazel Scott in *The Heat's On* (1943).

Miss Beavers and Bing Crosby in *Blue Skies* (1946).

(c)

(A) Ernest Whitman and
Ben Carter in *Maryland*
(1940). (B) Ernest
Whitman watches Jackie
Cooper and Henry Fonda
in *The Return of Frank
James* (1940). (C) Butter-
fly McQueen, Joann Marlowe,
Joan Crawford in *Mildred
Pierce* (1945). (D) Robert
Sterling, and Ernest Whit-
man in *The Getaway*
(1941). (E) Eddie Ander-
son, Ethel Waters, and
Paul Robeson in the
sharecropper segment, of
Tales of Manhattan (1942).
(F) Dooley Wilson sings
"As Time Goes By" to
Bogart in *Casablanca*
(1942).

135

Avon Long in the "Cinderella Sue" number from *Centennial Summer* (1946).

Canada Lee and Walter Slezak in *Lifeboat* (1944).

Billie Holiday and Dorothy Patrick in *New Orleans* (1947).

Clarence Muse played Marlene Dietrich's footman in *Flame of New Orleans* (1941)

Theresa Harris played Dietrich's maid in the same film.

Marietta Canty was the maid in *The Spoilers* (1943).

Ethel Waters in *Stage Door Canteen* (1943).

The Unconquered (1947) between Gary Cooper and Mike Mazurki.

Looking down at Leon Errol in *Hurry, Charlie, Hurry* (1941).

With Edgar Barrier and John Loder in *A Game of Death* (1945).

With Philip Reed in *Aloma of the South Seas* (1941).

The Desert Song (1943) between Irene Manning and Bruce Cabot.

(A) *They Got Me Covered* (1943), caught in a blackout with Bob Hope, Etta McDaniel, Ray Turner and Lenore Aubert. (B) Clarence Muse and Edward G. Robinson in *Scarlet Street* (1945). (C) Muse with Charles Boyer in *Flesh and Fantasy*. (D) Muse with Fred Astaire in *The Sky's the Limit* (1943). (E) Jeni LeGon between Ann Miller and Fred Astaire in *Easter Parade* (1948). (F) Hattie McDaniel in *Since You Went Away* (1944), with Joseph Cotten, Jennifer Jones and Claudette Colbert. (G) Rita Christiani (in the window) in the "Ice Cold Katie" number from *Thank Your Lucky Stars* (1943), with Hattie McDaniel and Willie Best.

(C)

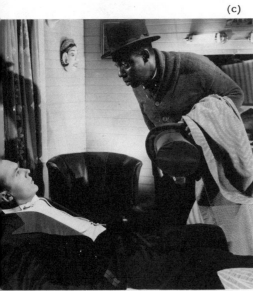

(D)

(E)

(F)

Ella Fitzgerald and the Merry Macs in *Ride 'Em Cowboy* (1942).

"Sir Lancelot" strums his guitar in *Brute Force* (1947).

The *Porgy and Bess* excerpt from *Rhapsody in Blue* (1945), with Madame Sul-te-wan and Anne Brown.

(Left) Canada Lee in *Body and Soul* (1947).

Gene Kelly and the Nicholas Brothers
in *The Pirate* (1949), "Be a Clown."

Hattie McDaniel and Bette Davis in *The Great Lie* (1940).

Lillian Yarbo and Gene Tierney in *The Return of Frank James* (1940)

Lillian Randolph standing next to Myrna Loy in *The Bachelor and the Bobby-Soxer* (1947).

More maids from the 1940's

Lillian Randolph takes James Stewart's hat in *It's a Wonderful Life* (1946).

Ruby Dandridge (Dorothy Dandridge's mother) with Lizabeth Scott in *Dead Reckoning* (1947).

Black Animated Characters

Jasper.

Eightball appeared in Universal cartoons.

From a George Pal Puppetoon film.

MGM's *Uncle Tom's Cabaña* (1947).

(A)

(B)

(A) June Haver and Betty Grable in *The Dolly Sisters* (1945).
(B) Eddie Foy Jr. and Bing Crosby in *Dixie* (1943). (C) Crosby and Marjorie Reynolds in *Holiday Inn* (1942). (D) Betty Grable doing "Lulu from Louisville" in *Coney Island* (1943). (E) Larry Parks as Al Jolson (1946). (F) Eddie Cantor sings "Dinah" in *Show Business* (1944).

(F)

(E)

(D)

(C)

Blackface in the 1940's

151

The Black Independents in the 1940's

A poster for *Miracle in Harlem* (1947).

From *Boy, What a Girl* (1946).

Louis Jordan and his saxophone in *Beware* (1947).

Moon Over Harlem

All-Negro Cast Films

BIG TIMERS
Stepin Fetchit in a mix-up with a chamber maid.
44 minutes $10

THE BLOOD OF JESUS
Undoubtedly the most powerful All-Negro motion picture ever produced. A great religious epic.
60 minutes $15

BROKEN STRINGS
Clarence Muse appears as a famous violinist who overcomes adversity with his son's help.
70 minutes $15

BRONZE BUCKAROO
Herbert Jeffrey and the Four Tones. Another fine Western with an all-star cast.
60 minutes $15

DARK MANHATTAN
Ralph Cooper stars in this smashing underworld drama.
66 minutes $15

THE DEVIL'S DAUGHTER
Nina Mae McKinney, Hamtree Harrington. A burning drama of love and hate in the tropics.
70 minutes $15

DOUBLE DEAL
Monte Hawley, Jeni Legon. Florence (Sulumai) O'Brien. His best pal gives him a double deal.
70 minutes $15

THE EXILE
Stanley Murrell and an all-star cast.
70 minutes $15

GANG WAR
Ralph Cooper.
See this machine gun thriller.
70 minutes $15

GO DOWN DEATH
Saturday sinners and Sunday saints clash in the battle of Good against Evil.
70 minutes $15

HARLEM BIG SHOT
A. B. Comethiere and Lorenzo Tucker "the Negro Valentino."
70 minutes

HARLEM IS HEAVEN
Bill Robinson
A fun-fest of joy, with Eubie Blake Orchestra.
70 minutes

GOD'S STEPCHILDREN
From the story "Naomi, Negress," of baby that looks white.

IT HAPPENED IN HARLEM
The owner of the Paradise Cafe finds a new singing star at the drug store.
30 minutes

LYING LIPS
Edna Mae Harris and an all-star cast.
70 minutes

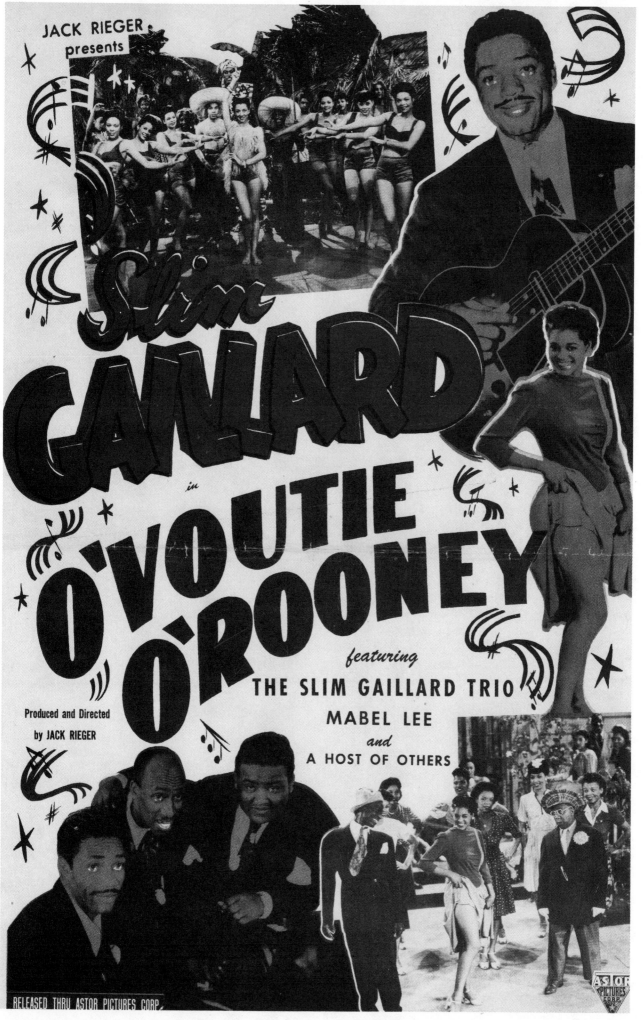

Poster from a be-bop movie, *O'Voutie O'Rooney* (1946).

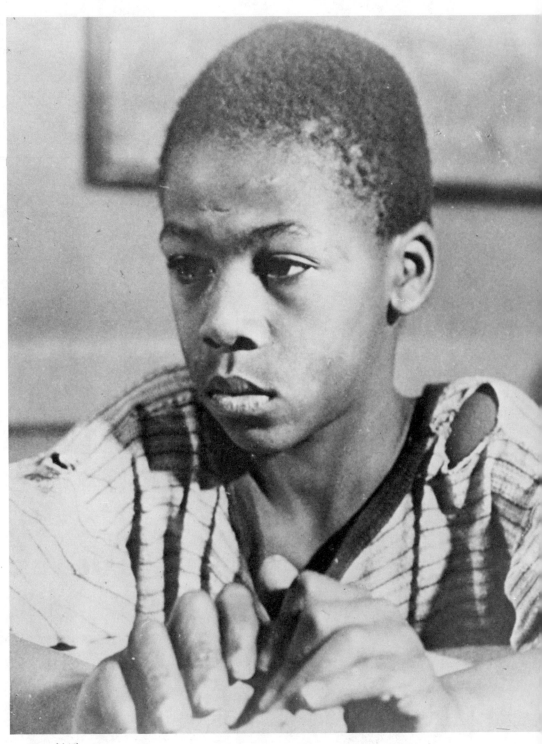

Donald Thompson.

Estelle Evans.

Chapter 5
The Fifties

During the fifties, racial identity and race relations, which had begun to be hinted at in the late forties, were portrayed on the screen and discussed more openly. Even more important, black actors and actresses acquired a new dignity, portraying recognizable, human people with whom audiences, white as well as black, could identify. White audiences were confronted by images of blacks that challenged their old assumptions.

Some of the performers who gained prominence in the fifties, including Sidney Poitier, Dorothy Dandridge, Eartha Kitt, Harry Belafonte, and several others, contributed to a changed view of the relationships of blacks and whites in society. Some of the films of the fifties, such as Richard Wright's *Native Son* (1951), *Cry, the Beloved Country* (1952), and *Something of Value* (1957), dealt with issues that had never been given serious consideration before. Blacks and whites began teaming up together in films like *Edge of the City* (1957) and *The Defiant Ones* (1958).

Despite these advances, many clichés lingered, in society and on the screen, especially in the all-black musicals. And mulatto roles were still played by whites

in the new *Show Boat* (1951), *Night of the Quarter Moon* (1959), and the 1959 remake of *Imitation of Life.*

The third movie version of *Show Boat,* in 1951, was essentially the same as previous versions, except that new cinematic techniques made it more spectacular.

Kathryn Grayson starred as Magnolia, Ava Gardner played the mulatto Julie, and William Warfield and Francis Williams portrayed Joe and Queenie, in the roles Paul Robeson and Hattie McDaniel had played so well in the 1936 version.

Hollywood was obviously still locked into safe, commercially successful images of blacks. Nevertheless, films now began, tentatively, to reflect the changing attitudes of society toward race and the more positive image blacks began to have of themselves.

In Richard Wright's 1951 film version of his novel *Native Son,* Bigger Thomas is the first explicitly rebellious black to come out of Hollywood. The film's subject matter made it an important movie, although poor acting and directing caused it to lose much of the urgency of the original book.

Wright himself played Bigger Thomas, the

Richard Wright (center) played Bigger Thomas in the film of his book *Native Son* (1950).

Wright on the fire escape in the film.

sensitive and intelligent rebel whose chances of success were thwarted, as Wright pointed out, from the moment he was born. Starting out as an idealist who wanted to help his fellow blacks, Thomas has been embittered by the exploitation and injustice of white prejudice. Unable to come to terms with the complexities and confusions of his life, he plans a robbery with some friends but begs off at the last moment because he is afraid of repercussions. Later he accidentally smothers his employer's daughter and desperately tries to cover up because "all my life I heard of black men being killed because of white girls."

From this point on, all the frustration, fear, and anguish come to the surface as he goes into hiding in the heart of the Chicago tenements—and within himself. Having failed with a ploy to ransom the supposedly kidnapped heiress, he escapes with his black girlfriend, whom he later kills because he believes she has led the police to his hiding place.

Whatever the drawbacks of this film, it attempted to show the effect of white bigotry on blacks and the impossibility of escaping the consequences.

Dorothy Dandridge as a schoolteacher and Philip Hepburn in *Bright Road* (1953).

Audience identification with characters is probably the most important way in which films can influence attitudes and help bring about social change. In the fifties, filmmakers attempted to reverse the negative images through which blacks had so long been portrayed and to present "real" individuals. There was now an attempt to overcompensate for the previous inadequacy of black roles.

Thus, Sidney Poitier became the new image of the middle-class black. Too good an actor ever to allow his portrayal of the parts (ninety percent of which, early in his career, put him in society's most respected occupations) to become two-dimensional, he seemed to believe that this image was the only way to combat racism. Indeed, this method did initially help to break down prejudice. Later, Poitier was to accept roles with which blacks, too, could identify.

Poitier's first leading role was in *No Way Out* a

1950 production by Darryl F. Zanuck. As the only nonwhite intern in a large metropolitan hospital, Poitier, as Dr. Luther Brooks, is subjected to insults and humiliation from his medical colleagues as well as the patients. When a man whom Poitier suspected to have been wrongly diagnosed dies while Poitier is preparing to operate on him, the man's brother, a violent racist played by Richard Widmark, starts a campaign against the "black killer." Widmark refuses to allow Poitier to perform an autopsy, which would prove his innocence, and instead plans a riot at the hospital. Finally, however, Poitier convinces everyone of his innocence.

Poitier is always pictured as calm and patient with all his patients, and his medical ability is impeccable. If he does not convince all his colleagues of his competence, at least he gets them to accept having a black doctor work on white as well as black patients. As

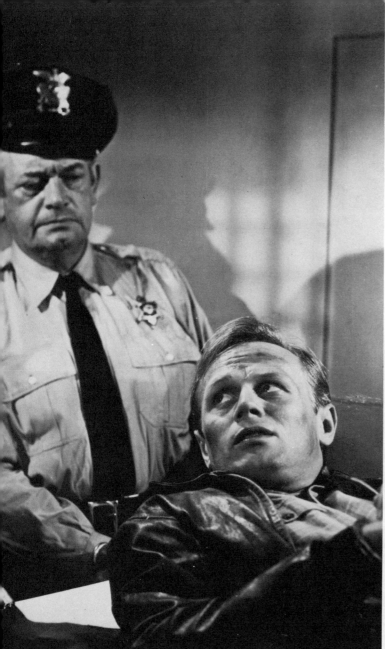

Sidney Poitier and Richard Widmark in *No Way Out* (1950).

Poitier with Glenn Ford in *Blackboard Jungle* (1955).

the dedicated, civilized professional he gives a dignified performance that was to become almost his trademark.

Dorothy Dandridge also plays a professional, a schoolteacher, in *Bright Road* an MGM production of 1953. This almost all-black film has a brief appearance by one white man, a doctor, but otherwise concerns itself solely with black problems.

A young student (Philip Hepburn) is the victim of racial discrimination, a troubled home life, and unhappiness due to the death of a schoolmate. In attempting to communicate with him, Dandridge reveals the calm compassion and warmth that seem to be the mark of the "new Negro" in fifties movies.

Unfortunately, for all its good intentions the film suffers from a weak script by Emmet Lavery, who either could not or did not want to show the boy's background in a light that would have made his bitterness

comprehensible. The school he goes to is all black, there are no scenes of racial discrimination, his home turns out to be relatively untroubled, and the dead girl was really not a friend at all. Except for a few poignant scenes between Dandridge and the boy, the film is rather pointless.

This was also Harry Belafonte's debut, an unimpressive portrayal of the school principal.

The new black actors did not exclusively portray doctors and lawyers by any means. One of Poitier's best films, one of the best films of the fifties, is *Blackboard Jungle* (1955), in which he played the role of a tough high school kid.

Blackboard Jungle was a realistic drama of urban school life. Poitier, as the most interesting student, is like the others, hard as nails, with complete contempt for Glenn Ford, the teacher. The film traces the gradual emergence of Poitier's compassion for Ford. The climax

Peggy Dow, Richard Egan, James Edwards, Arthur Kennedy and Murray Hamilton in *Bright Victory* (1951).

James Edwards with Robert Ryan in *Men in War* (1957).

comes when Vic Morrow, as the toughest kid, threatens the teacher with a knife and Poitier, who has made the transition from hating the whole system to feeling sympathy for the teacher's position, steps between the two to break up the fight and snatch the knife from Morrow's hands. This scene was so well played that audiences were electrified. The film was a landmark and did a great deal to enhance Poitier's career.

Another actor who appeared in *Blackboard Jungle* was Rafael Campos. He and Juano Hernandez both played important roles in *Trial* (1955), a film about how prejudice in a small California town impedes justice. Campos plays an innocent Mexican boy accused of assaulting a white girl who subsequently died of a heart attack. Unfortunately, Don Mankiewicz, who wrote the script, complicated the plot with an anti-Communist subplot in the form of the boy's lawyer, a wily Communist who is attempting to use the case for political purposes. Glenn Ford, as the lawyer, was unable to act competently owing to the cliché-ridden dialogue. Juano Hernandez portrayed the black judge. The townspeople are presented as irrational and unfeeling bigots who demand the youth's lynching before the trial.

In *The Well* (1951), in which a young black boy is trapped in a mine shaft and a white bigot is asked to save him, Hollywood had a good opportunity to make a serious comment on the race question. Instead, the producers chose to avoid the issue, for after the initial scenes, the boy's color became unimportant. The film turned into a rather poor documentary about the hazards of mines. For those who wished to notice it, the theme of a racist saving a black child was secondary.

Another film that avoided the issue of racism was *Bright Victory* (1951), in which a blinded war veteran (Arthur Kennedy) is befriended by another disabled vet played by black actor James Edwards. The main story is romantic, but in the subplot the race issue is treated ambivalently. The attitude seems to be that it takes a blind man to transcend the color line. Vague allusions are made to the importance of companionship, and blindness is treated in a reverential way as bringing true wisdom.

Three films of the fifties dealt with a new subject, black roots. Previously, with rare exceptions, any depiction of Africa had shown blacks only as savages. *The Emperor Jones* had done something to change that, but *Cry, the Beloved Country* was the first film to try to present a realistic picture of African life.

Cry, the Beloved Country was directed by Zoltan Korda, and the script was adapted by Alan Paton from his bestselling book. Set in a South African village torn

Sidney Poitier and Canada Lee in Alexander Korda's British-made version of *Cry, the Beloved Country* (1951).

Dane Clark, Sidney Poitier, and Ruby Dee in *Go Man Go* (1954).

The Well (1951), Richard Rober, George Hamilton, Madie Norman, Ernest Anderson.

Frederick O'Neal, Juano Hernandez and Sidney Poitier in *Something of Value* (1959).

by racial strife, this film is considered one of the best black movies ever made. Unlike most of the contemporary films on the subject, *Cry, the Beloved Country* never wavers from its theme—that through grief and suffering society may purge itself of the hate, fear, and ignorance that cause prejudice. It treats the subject with an unrelenting compassion. As Bosley Crowther said in *The New York Times*, the story is

> the dark and terrible passage of two men through the valley of grief and distraction into which they are plunged by a mutually calamitous act. One is a simple, God-fearing Negro Anglican priest who comes down from the sturdy hills of Natal to Johannesburg to seek his sister and his missing son and who arrives too late to save the lost lad from murdering a respected white man. And the other is the father of the white man murdered by the old priest's son—a rich and bigoted farmer.

Enough of the slum conditions of black Johannesburg is shown to suggest the background to the murder, but the main emphasis is on the relationship between the two men. Canada Lee, as the old Zulu priest, and Charles Carson, as the white father, simultaneously come to the conclusion that harmony must prevail between their races if the world is to survive. Their conflict becomes a microcosm of all such conflicts everywhere.

The brilliance with which Korda and Paton put this film together gave universality to a story with a local theme. The situation and its attendant tragedy could have taken place in New York or Alabama as well as in Africa.

Cry, the Beloved Country was the last film Canada Lee made.

Something of Value (1957) also featured conflict between a black man and a white man, this time childhood friends. Director Richard Brooks was attempting an adaptation of Robert Ruark's bloody novel of the Mau Mau uprising in Kenya, but he managed to sentimentalize a great part of it.

Sidney Poitier, as a follower of the Mau Mau chieftain (Juano Hernandez), must fight Rock Hudson, his former friend, to the death. Poitier and Hernandez both give strong performances, but Hudson and Dana Wynter (as his fiancée) seem strangely out of place.

Something of Value, a basically white-oriented film, concentrated on the savagery of the Mau Mau while purporting to explain the injustices that led to the uprising. Poitier and Hernandez possess a kind of dignity in their roles that makes Hudson's heavy posturing as the just white man seem weak by comparison. However, the film is ambivalent; it pays tribute to the African way of life, but it also represents the natives as primitives who appear to enjoy mutilating the bodies of animals and white men.

A third black-roots film was *Tamango* (1959), with Curt Jurgens, Dorothy Dandridge, and Jean Servais. There is some very fine acting in this story of a slave trader's voyage from Africa to Cuba, but in trying to humanize the trader (Jurgens), the film failed to produce any insight into one of the most significant voyages the black people made.

Contemporary black life was represented on the screen with the appearance of black athletes in documentaries about their lives. The first athlete to appear on the screen was Jackie Robinson, who had broken the color bar in baseball by playing with the Brooklyn Dodgers.

In *The Jackie Robinson Story* (1950), scriptwriters Lawrence Taylor and Arthur Mann gave the star minimal dialogue for fear that he would not come off well. This was a mistake, since even an experienced actor will have a hard task performing a role without words to back up the emotions he must portray. Robinson, though not an actor, managed to

Jackie Robinson (in his only film) with Louise Beavers in *The Jackie Robinson Story* (1950).

Curt Jurgens embraces Dorothy Dandridge in *Tamango* (1957).

play his part expertly and with a dignity that showed his control and his ability to handle a situation with minimal difficulty.

The president of the Dodgers, Branch Rickey, portrayed in the film by Minor Watson, lets Robinson know what he may have to face and informs him that he must not fight back; he must just play good ball. This is what the rest of the film is about, and Robinson's performance must have been the envy of many Hollywood actors.

Inspired by this film, *The Joe Louis Story* followed in 1953. Coley Wallace, a professional heavyweight boxer, made his screen debut as the champion and lent a great deal of authenticity to his part, especially since he looked like Louis.

The third fifties sports film was *The Harlem Globetrotters* with the famous basketball team aided by Dorothy Dandridge and Bill Walker. Though it was intended purely as entertainment and did little to advance the cause of civil rights, the film was amusing and informative.

A number of films made in the fifties and early sixties were based on the lives of various jazz musicians. Starting with *The Glenn Miller Story* (1954), Hollywood went on to produce *St. Louis Blues* (1958), *Odds against Tomorrow* (1959), and *All the Fine Young Cannibals* (1960). All these films except the last rely heavily on musicianship and appear to pay homage to the "natural rhythm of the blacks" theme.

In *St. Louis Blues,* the preacher father of the film's star, Nat King Cole, is shown throwing his son's cornet under the wheels of a wagon. Ruby Dee, advocate of "the Lord's music," and Eartha Kitt, with her penchant for "the devil's music," join Ella Fitzgerald, Pearl Bailey, and Mahalia Jackson in belting out their favorite numbers to a parade of stars like Cab Calloway, Juano Hernandez, and Billy Preston while Cole occupies himself with being a frustrated composer. In sacrificing the plot to the music, the writers made a wise move, for the music makes this film successful.

The Glenn Miller Story, unlike the other jazz films, is not specifically black. In it, Louis Armstrong teams up with Gene Krupa in a freewheeling rendition of "Basin Street Blues."

Odds against Tomorrow starred Harry Belafonte as a nightclub musician who turns to crime. Motivation is not the strong point of this film, for why Belafonte turns to crime is never really explained. He has gambling debts, which give a superficial reason, but the audience is never given a satisfactory explanation. The suggestion is that here is the black man forced by circumstances into stealing from the society that made him that way.

(A)

(B)

(c)

(D)

In *All the Fine Young Cannibals,* singer Pearl
Bailey portrays Ruby Jones, a jazz and blues singer of
the twenties in her decline and on the skids. The film
tries hard to capture the period rhythm, but the plot is
contrived. A varied collection of people mill around
Miss Bailey as she trots from her bedroom to the club.
Pearl Bailey is fine as the singer, however, and her
funeral exalts the Negro race as the "force of rhythm"
in the music world.

Scenes from Carmen Jones
(1954)

A romantic interval.

Miss Dandridge with Brock Peters.

Harry Belafonte admiring Miss Dandridge.

The premise that blacks have natural rhythm ensured the popularity of all-black movies, which continued to appear in the fifties. These films were mere showcases for the talents of various performers and were responsible for maintaining black stereotypes. But they made money for the major studios and started many blacks on careers they might not otherwise have had. Generally speaking, the acting and singing were exceptionally good.

Of the more important musicals of this genre, Otto Preminger's screen version of *Carmen Jones,* Oscar Hammerstein's updated, hip version of Bizet's *Carmen,* was the most successful. In *Carmen Jones,* Carmen has become a worker in a parachute factory. Played by the dynamic Dorothy Dandridge, she causes Joe, formerly Don José, a student air force pilot, to go AWOL for love of her. However, just as Bizet's Carmen did, she tires of Joe and runs off with Husky Miller the prize fighter, the modern version of Escamillo the matador.

Harry Belafonte gave a strong performance as Joe. Dorothy Dandridge, as Carmen, was nominated for an Academy Award for best actress, the first time a black actress had been nominated.

Dorothy Dandridge's career began in 1941, with a role in *Lady From Louisiana,* and lasted twenty years, culminating in *Malaga* in 1962, the year of her premature death. Bosley Crowther described her role in Carmen Jones as "a slinky, hip-swinging main-drag beauty with a slangy, come-hither way with men. . . . This cool, calculating little siren seems mainly interested in having a good time."

In fact, the role Dandridge plays in *Carmen Jones* and later in *Porgy and Bess* does not essentially depart from the image of the mulatto woman whose white blood makes her beautiful and whose black blood degrades her and who is doomed to die tragically, as Nina Mae McKinney did in *Hallelujah* and Fredi Washington should have in *Imitation of Life.* In Hollywood, right up to the present, the beautiful black

Harry Belafonte and Dorothy Dandridge.

Scenes from
Porgy and Bess
(1959)

(A) Brock Peters, Sidney Poitier and
Dorothy Dandridge. (B) Porgy and Bess
(Poitier and Dandridge).

woman has always been light-skinned and short-lived.

The other major black musical of the fifties was, of course *Porgy and Bess,* which appeared in 1959. This was another Preminger movie with Sidney Poitier as Porgy, Dorothy Dandridge as Bess, and Pearl Bailey, Brock Peters, and Sammy Davis, Jr., playing the other leads.

The action takes place on Charleston's Catfish Row, where the Negroes sing, fight, pick cotton, shoot craps, and idle away their days. Bess, the beautiful child-woman of an escaped murderer, Crown (Brock Peters), seeks refuge with Porgy, the drunken cripple who is the brunt of all the jokers on Catfish Row. Despite her erratic nature and the temptations of Sportin' Life (Davis), who offers her "happy dust" and a life with him in New York, Bess grows to love her Porgy, who in return tries to reform her. However, one stormy night, Crown returns to get Bess, and Porgy kills him. The police come to investigate, and they take Porgy away to identify the body. Being a superstitious Southern Negro, Porgy refuses to look at the body and is finally released after a short stay in prison. He returns home, to find that the despairing Bess has gone to New York with Sportin' Life. Nonetheless, Porgy calls for his pathetic little goat cart and rides north after his woman.

(c) Dorothy Dandridge with Sammy
Davis, Jr., as Sportin' Life. (d) Diahann
Carroll and Pearl Bailey. (e) Dorothy
Dandridge, Clarence Muse and Poitier.

Porgy and Bess first appeared on Broadway in
1927. It was presented as an opera in 1935 with George
Gershwin's music, and this is the version Preminger
adapted for his film. The music and dance sequences
are very good, but *Porgy and Bess* was criticized by
black journalists for pandering to the old "darkie"
images. Poitier to this day regrets having accepted his
part. In her biography of Poitier, Carolyn H. Ewers
quotes him as saying,

> I hated doing *Porgy and Bess*, but pressure was
> brought to bear from a number of quarters
> and there was a threat of my career stopping
> dead still. I toyed with the idea of being
> steadfast, but I weakened ultimately and did
> it. I didn't enjoy doing it, and I have not yet
> completely forgiven myself.

(A)

(B)

(A) Rex Ingram and Eartha Kitt in *Anna Lucasta* (1959). (B) Sammy Davis, Jr., makes Anna Lucasta (Eartha Kitt) laugh. (C) Eartha Kitt sings "Monotonous" in *New Faces* (1954).

(C)

Like Dorothy Dandridge, Pearl Bailey, and Lena Horne, Eartha Kitt was a singer turned actress whose light skin earned her sex-siren roles in films. Her first film, *New Faces* (1954), was a review that introduced other performers who later came to prominence, such as Paul Lynde, Carol Lawrence, and Robert Clary. Of all the performers, Miss Kitt got the most admiring reviews for her singing of "Uskadara," "C'est Si Bon," and "Santa Baby." Her later films included *The Mark of the Hawk* (1958), *St. Louis Blues* (1958), *Anna Lucasta* (1959), and *Synanon* (1965).

Anna Lucasta was a particularly ludicrous vehicle for Eartha Kitt's portrayal of a "prostitute with a heart of gold" who is driven to her life of sin by her clownish father (Rex Ingram), spends a romantic interlude with Sammy Davis, Jr., and then reforms to marry a decent farm boy.

(Overleaf) *Member of the Wedding* (1952): Julie Harris, Ethel Waters, James Edwards and Brandon De Wilde.

Sidney Poitier and Tony Curtis in *The Defiant Ones* (1958).

From the 1959 *Imitation of Life*: Juanita Moore with Karen Dicker and Terry Burnham.

The more decorous black-mammy figure of long Hollywood tradition became something of an earth-mother with Ethel Waters's roles in two well-received fifties films. *Member of the Wedding,* based on a novel and a play by Carson McCullers, appeared in 1952 and was followed by *The Sound and the Fury* in 1959.

Member of the Wedding is a restrained story of an adolescent girl growing up lonely in a small Southern town. Julie Harris, as the young girl, owes her development primarily to the influence of the strong, warm-hearted Berenice. Bosley Crowther wrote of Ethel Waters's performance in this role,

> Ethel Waters' performance as the mammy repeated on the screen in a manner indistinguishable from her delivery of it on the stage, glows with a warmth of personality and understanding that transmits a wonderful incidental concept of the pathos of the transient nurse.

In the film adaptation of Faulkner's novel *The Sound and the Fury,* Ethel Waters's Dilsey is no ordinary servant. The only strong member of a decaying, aristocratic white Southern family, she holds them all together with her dignity and strength. It is she who sees that Benji, the half-vegetal brother of Jason (Yul Brynner) is fed and dressed and gets to town when necessary. She offers advice to the rest of the family and they take it. As Faulkner said, Dilsey is the nexus of the family, and Ethel Waters's performance is definitive.

Blackface, another outmoded Hollywood tradition, was also still around in the fifties. For instance, light-skinned black actress Ellen Holly was considered for the part of the daughter in the 1959 remake of *Imitation of Life* but lost it to Susan Kohner because producers thought Miss Holly would not have the drawing power of a white actress.

In *Kings Go Forth* (1958) Natalie Wood stars as Monique Blain, a girl who is discovered to have Negro blood but with whom Frank Sinatra falls in love. Julie London is one-quarter Negro in *Night of the Quarter Moon* (1959), a rather dismal effort to portray racial harmony in a melodramatic film about a happy ever-so-slightly interracial marriage that selfish in-laws attempt to break up.

Two controversial films of the late fifties portrayed racial brotherhood in a meaningful way. In *Edge of the City* John Cassavetes, as the hobo, comes to work with black Tommy Tyler (Sidney Poitier) on a construction gang. Vanning, the hobo, prefers to work with Poitier rather than with the white boss (Jack Warden). Befriended by his partner, Vanning goes home with him to meet his wife and daughter. Vanning is confronted by the wife (Ruby Dee) after her husband has died defending him. Because Vanning is the hero of the film, he must avenge his black brother's death. One must ask, why is it necessary for Poitier to die?

Poitier dies for one white man in *Edge of the City* and sacrifices his freedom for another in *The Defiant Ones.* From today's standpoint, Poitier's nobility looks Uncle Tomish. In the context of the fifties, however, the noble dignified black man was a new departure from old images.

The Defiant Ones focuses on the unwilling partnership of two men who consider themselves separate and share a mutual hostility based on race. Poitier and Tony Curtis, convicts who escape chained together from a prison gang, run together through swamps and fields and gradually go through a transformation that turns them from enemies into friends as they come to realize through mutual dependence that they are brothers under the skin. In the last scene, as they have the opportunity of escape on a passing freight train, Curtis falls, unable to make it, and Poitier simply jumps back down to be with his friend as the posse closes in.

From today's perspective these two films may seem somewhat hackneyed, but at the time they were innovative. They dealt with race relations in a far deeper way than the last black-oriented film of 1959, *The World, the Flesh and the Devil,* starring Harry Belafonte.

This film starts promisingly. An atomic war has destroyed the world, and Belafonte is walking through the empty streets of New York searching for other survivors. It seems that there are only three people left in the world—Belafonte, Inger Stevens, and Mel Ferrer. One woman is caught between two men, one of whom is black. At this point, the film loses credibility, melodrama sets in, and the romantic triangle absorbs all else. The simplistic film ends with Ferrer challenging Belafonte to a duel, in which the black man is killed. A kind, compassionate black is sacrificed to make the world white again.

It is possible to be very cynical about such a film because it does not seem to question white supremacy. However, looking at the decade in which it was made, a marked change is discernible in black Hollywood. Old stereotypes are still present, but they are being questioned, and new discussions are being initiated

Jack Warden grapples with Sidney Poitier in *Edge of the City* (1957).

Harry Belafonte in *The World, The Flesh and the Devil* (1959).

between blacks and whites. The black heritage is considered interesting enough for several feature films. Superstars like Poitier and Belafonte have emerged, and there are the faint rustlings of a new militancy.

All these themes would be explored with greater perception and depth during the turbulent sixties.

(A)

(B)

(E)

178

(D)

(A) John Justin and Dorothy Dandridge. (B) Joan Fontaine dances with Harry Belafonte while James Mason guides Miss Dandridge. (C) Dorothy Dandridge and Harry Belafonte. (D) Stephen Boyd is flanked by Miss Dandridge and Joan Collins. (E) Joan Fontaine and Belafonte.

Chapter 6
The Sixties

The sixties were traumatic for America. The decade began in an atmosphere of hope and saw many solid, progressive goals achieved; yet the period seethed with violence, frustration, anger, and fear. It was a decade during which America was shocked out of its complacency by riots, political assassinations, and the brutality of the increasingly unpopular Vietnam war. Also, during this era race relations became the single most powerful cause, springing to the forefront of the nation's consciousness with an intensity stronger than at any time since Reconstruction.

Among the movie industry's efforts to chronicle race relations in this turbulent decade, failures abounded, but there were a handful of gems. Hollywood was clumsy in its handling of the abundant drama of the black movement. Even so, the position of the black actor improved significantly during the sixties. In what previous era could a black man have won the best-actor Oscar, as Sidney Poitier did for 1963? In what previous decade could a Gallup poll have revealed the startling discovery that this same actor had climbed in popularity to the very top?

The three earliest films about blacks in the decade were made with the intention of showing blacks in a good light. They point out Hollywood's tendency to be far more comfortable portraying superhuman absolutes than real people with real problems. Of the three, the two that succeeded as movies were *All the Young Men* (1960) and *Sergeant Rutledge* (1960), which were both less emotionally ambitious than *Take a Giant Step* (1961).

All the Young Men, starring Sidney Poitier, though didactic in spots, pumped effectively for racial tolerance. Written, produced, and directed by Hall Bartlett, it featured Alan Ladd, Mort Sahl, James Darren, and Ingmar Johansson.

The story dealt with a black sergeant, played by Poitier, in command of a squad of marines during the Korean war. In addition to challenges presented by the enemy, he had to cope with bigotry among the men. Ladd played a busted topkick, bitter and cynical. Characters included a bigoted Southerner, a wisecracking city boy, and an American Indian who allies himself with Poitier. They and the other players portrayed variations on the usual Hollywood soldier theme, with sweethearts at home, death, Communism,

(A) Constance Towers struggles for Jeffrey Hunter's rifle, while Juano Hernandez looks on, in *Sergeant Rutledge* (1959). (B) Woody Strode (center) as Sergeant Rutledge. (C) Frederick O'Neal and Estelle Hemsley as Johnny Nash's parents in *Take a Giant Step* (1961).

(B)

(C)

and the folks back on the farm figuring dutifully in the script. A gimmick popular in Westerns polished off the plot as the intrepid Poitier, though beleaguered by defection in the ranks, pulled through despite all odds, his brute courage dissolving resentment and hate. Thus, the story, though exciting in a traditional mold, was hardly an innovative breakthrough.

Sergeant Rutledge was also an army film, as were a majority of the movies made with black actors during the sixties. Perhaps Hollywood did not yet dare to chronicle the truly dramatic struggles of black civilian life. This film, directed by John Ford, exposed the prejudices of a hundred years ago. The period was post-Civil War; the setting, Arizona. Woody Strode was excellent as the black Sergeant Rutledge, who was accused of raping and strangling a white girl and of murdering her father, the commanding officer. Throughout the film it was obvious that the dignified Sergeant Rutledge was quite incapable of having committed such heinous crimes but equally obvious that his white accusers were eager to shut out any of their own doubts. The good sergeant was too stoically saintly for some tastes, but the film was thoughtful, well acted,

and not without dramatic bite.

Take a Giant Step, based on the play by Louis S. Peterson, featured Ruby Dee and Frederick O'Neal, along with Beah Richards and Johnny Nash. It depicted the problems of a black adolescent as he matured in a middle-class white community and attempted to deal with the problem of being black in a society that teaches one to hate blacks.

Scenes from
A Raisin In the Sun
(1961)

Sidney Poitier.   Ruby Dee and Poitier.

A cheerful moment: Ruby Dee, Diana Sands and Poitier are standing over the seated Claudia O'Neill.

The film dealt with the wounds that black men face in everyday life—wounds such as those caused realizing that the white kids, who just loved having the black boy on their baseball team, didn't want to associate with him off the playing field.

Unfortunately, despite its worthwhile goals, the film was too wary to tackle its controversial subject vigorously. As a result, the movie lacked the play's punch and made the boy's confusion over racial prejudice and his struggles against the sex urge seem at times like a cross between a social-justice brochure and a black Andy Hardy film. Unfortunately, the studio industry seems incapable of dealing head on with "sensitive" topics without smothering them in syrupy sentiment.

During the early sixties, civil rights claimed a major share of the public's attention. The growing militancy and awareness of blacks was channeled into the nonviolent activities championed by the Reverend Dr. Martin Luther King, Jr. These were years of growing moderation in the South and growing activity in the North. The Kennedy administration, though disappointing on some fronts, took vigorous action to expand equal employment opportunities, to protect voting rights, and to increase the number of blacks in important government posts.

The first really memorable film of the sixties made about blacks, *Raisin in the Sun* (1961), reflected this hopeful atmosphere. Columbia Pictures, which financed the film, knew that it was a risky project. Although Lorraine Hansberry's play, on which it was based, had won the New York Drama Critics Award, the film could be expected to make no money in the South and might be a flop abroad. The risk was taken because Columbia thought that it might prove to be a great film. This risk, so atypical of Hollywood's usual caution, is a testament both to the executives who took it and to the idealistic tenor of the times.

The film featured Sidney Poitier, Claudia McNeil, and Diana Sands in a story about a black family seeking to escape from a South Side Chicago tenement into the more wholesome environment of a suburb. The movie ably set forth the dignity, humor, and strength of the family as it tried to cope with life's uncertainties.

The film stuck faithfully to the script of the play, avoiding the temptation to hide the subject beneath Hollywood-style melodramatics and glitter but also unfortunately boxing it into the unnecessary limitations of the stage. *A Raisin in the Sun* was perhaps not a great film, but it was impressive enough to raise hopes that the cinema was going ahead with the long-neglected exposition of the black experience.

1961 also saw the release of several more films which sounded notes of hope on racial themes.

Paul Newman, a good friend of Sidney Poitier, had always taken interest in liberal causes. In fact, during the sixties he and such stars as Marlon Brando visited various Southern cities to protest their racial injustices. In 1961 he, Poitier, Joanne Woodward, and Diahann Carroll starred in *Paris Blues,* a film about the lives and loves of two American jazz musicians living in Paris. Though wandering and unclear, this film made the point that a man must find his battle and fight it. Newman decides to stay in Paris and take up the challenge of building a serious career, though it means the loss of Miss Woodward, who returns to the States. Poitier eventually realizes that despite his severe disillusionment with racial conditions in the United States, his fight is to change them. The first-rate musicianship of Louis Armstrong gave a much-needed lift to a movie that at times got lost amidst its ramblings.

That same year Roger Corman directed *The Intruder,* based on a novel by Charles Beaumont. The story involved an anti-integrationist who goes to a small town in the South to rouse the people against school integration. The film highlighted the problems and pressures implicit in this tragic situation and concluded on a note of hope for wiser resolutions to the dilemmas.

An interesting 1961 film better known outside the United States than here is *The Young One,* directed by the renowned Spanish director Luis Buñuel. In this, Buñuel's first film about the United States, he dealt head on with the racial issue. The film starred Bernie Hamilton and Zachary Scott. The setting is an isolated island over which Scott, in the company of a thirteen-year-old girl, serves as warden. The black Hamilton has been accused, probably unjustly, of raping a white woman, and he seeks refuge on the island. In dealing with the white warden's jealousy of the young girl's interest in the black stranger, the film deals with race on a man-to-man basis. Being isolated from society, the warden has no one to support him in the troublesome job of putting the black man "in his place."

It is surprising that this sophisticated film is so little known in the United States, even among people especially interested in films about blacks.

Probably the least-known film to feature blacks in 1961 was Jonas Mekas's independently made experimental film *Guns of the Trees.* It featured camera and sound effects joined in clever simulation of a drug experience, while giving insights into the lives of black and white married couples. It would be a few years before techniques and subjects of the New York "underground" would emerge, grabbed by a Hollywood desperate for the relevance that a new young audience wanted.

A comparison of some of the films released in 1962 points out how efforts at "educating" an audience can reduce a film's chance to reach the emotions.

Pressure Point, produced by Stanley Kramer and directed by Hubert Cornfield was an extreme example of the pitfalls of condescending moralization. In this story Bobby Darin portrays a psychopathic convict and vicious hater of Negroes and Jews, and Sidney Poitier portrays his unbelievably self-controlled black psychiatrist. The film was chopped up by confusing flashbacks, and though obviously sincere, it was almost

Gregory Peck as Brock Peters' attorney for the defense in *To Kill a Mocking Bird* (1962).

The story dealt with the problems faced by Peck, as a white Southern lawyer with noble instincts, who takes on the unpopular defense of a black farmer accused of raping a white girl. The film supplied good parts for Brock Peters, as the farmer, and Estelle Evans, as the lawyer's strong-minded servant, Calpurnia. These roles were based on flesh-and-blood characters, just as the entire movie was based on a true story. The film's realism made it an outstanding landmark for Hollywood.

To Kill a Mockingbird was generally considered a fine film and lauded for its indictment of bigotry; yet some radical critics tended to question the "great white father" image presented by Gregory Peck, who said that one of his motives for making the film was to reveal overseas a portrait of the responsible and moderate South.

Meanwhile, interracial love was the subject of England's Continental Pictures *A Taste of Honey* (1962). Tony Richardson, who directed, and Shelagh Delaney, who adapted the script from her well-received play, seemed far less intimidated than their American counterparts. Instead of stuffing their black character into a tightly fitting role as a symbol of heroism, villainy, or anything else, they simply gave him room to breathe. The character, a young black sailor, is shown as a rather ordinary person involved in everyday life, a man who, just like everyone else, is capable of helping, hurting, and making mistakes.

The sailor becomes involved with a lonely young white girl during his shore leave and returns to his ship unaware that she is pregnant with his child. The focus is on the sorrows and limitations of the girl's life in a grim northern-English city slum. Her lover's race is mentioned no more nor less than it would be in reality. The interference of the girl's crude and unfeeling mother is seen to be as much of a problem to her as the color of her baby will be.

1963 brought the release of *Lilies of the Field*, for which Sidney Poitier won the best-actor Oscar, becoming the first black so honored. This film was a modest modern parable about a migrant construction worker who is wooed to the work of God, building a chapel, by the mother superior of a group of Arizona-based Teutonic nuns.

The film, produced on a very low budget by United Artists, was made possible almost entirely through the efforts of those who worked on it. Its director, Ralph Nelson, risked his future by promising to shoot it in fourteen and a half days or to pay the overtime out of his own pocket. Both its scriptwriter and Poitier agreed to accept wages far below their usual prices, augmented only by percentages in the

totally misguided. Darin, a former member of the American Nazi party, represented pure evil in contrast to Poitier's ideal liberal man. The picture concentrated on a strictly delineated struggle between good and evil that seemed to have no remote relation to anything human. It was too busy teaching the audience that racial hatred isn't nice even to touch upon the potentially fascinating subject of how the psychiatrist, as a man, felt.

Convicts Four, produced by A. Ronald Lubin, was another movie filled with good intentions but hardly believable results. Sammy Davis, Jr., plays the color-conscious cell mate of Ben Gazzara, a murderer. The plot details Gazzara's reprieve from execution and his subsequent rehabilitation and release due to his artistic talents. Any constructive elements in the film were totally lost in an embarrassing plot and flat characterizations.

Davis appeared again in 1962, in the rather baffling role of a fawning ex-slave in *Sergeants Three*. This film, which starred Frank Sinatra, Dean Martin, and Peter Lawford as members of a U.S. cavalry unit on the Western frontier, was an adventure spoof centered more around various nightclub routines than around history. As such, it provided infinitely more fun than the two aforementioned message movies of the year.

A film that managed to execute more serious intentions very successfully was Universal International's *To Kill a Mockingbird*, produced by Alan J. Pakula and directed by Robert Mulligan. Based on Harper Lee's Pulitzer Prize-winning novel, it starred Gregory Peck, whose performance won him the 1962 Academy Award for best actor in a leading role.

(A)

film, which they fully expected to make little or no money. The entire cast and crew worked for minimum wages and managed to muster so much enthusiasm for the project that the shooting was actually finished half a day under its preposterously short schedule.

The result of this labor of love was one of the warmest films ever to appear on the commercial circuit.

Among the films with racial themes released in 1964, the three that stand out as the best were produced on extremely low budgets. These were *Nothing but a Man, The Cool World,* and the slightly less impressive *One Potato, Two Potato.*

The independently made *Nothing but a Man* won considerable praise for avoiding sentimentality and simply telling it "like it is." This film, which starred Ivan Dixon and Abbey Lincoln, poignantly depicts the efforts of Dixon, as a black laborer, to come to terms with both the good and the bad aspects of his life. The film deals with the problems of being "nothing but a man," problems made harder because that man is black. The characters speak for themselves, without moralizing.

Another exceptional independently made film of that year was Shirley Clark's *The Cool World.* Based on Warren Miller's novel, it focused on the criminal

adventures of a youth who aspires to and briefly achieves the chieftancy of a Harlem gang. The film was cinematically innovative, and its spontaneity and realistic tenor were aided because most of its actors had little or no acting experience.

Full of vicious and hideous truths, it managed to offend *The New York Times'* critic Bosley Crowther, who otherwise considered it an excellent film, with its "too free use of four-letter words."

One Potato, Two Potato dealt with the injustices arising from an interracial love affair. Barbara Barrie plays a white divorcée, and Bernie Hamilton plays her black lover, determined to let no obstacles stand in the way of their marriage. Despite some discomforting sentimentality, performances were moving and believable, and the direction and plot were professional and smooth.

A number of less distinguished movies about blacks were made during that year of overwhelming concern about civil rights.

James Whitmore did a variation on the blackface routine, this time in a serious vein, in the Walter Reade-Sterling production of *Black Like Me.* The story was based on the true experiences of a dedicated white journalist who, with the help of a special skin pigment

186

(c)

(d)

(B)

(A) Sidney Poitier impresses the sisters in
Lilies of the Field (1963). (B) Poitier
building a steeple in the same film. (C) *The
Cool World* (1963): Hampton Clanton
(center). (D) Barbara Barrie and Bernie
Hamilton in *One Potato, Two Potato*
(1964).

187

Jim Brown backs up Rod Taylor in *Dark of the Sun* (1968).

treatment, became dark enough to pass as a black and discover for himself what it feels like to be a modern-day "darkie" in the Deep South. Unfortunately melodrama took precedence over subtlety in the script, and the opportunity to explore a white man's sudden initiation into life as a black was wasted.

Johnny Cool was produced and directed by William Asher. Sammy Davis, Jr., played "Educated," a sophisticated hanger-on in the underworld's gambling casinos. Underworld life and intergang rivalry were shown throughout; though the doings smacked of run-of-mill gangster pictures and offered only a minimal racial emphasis, the action was sleek and fast.

Davis projected vitality and excitement. His resiliency in the face of obstacles, his hopes for the future, and his persistent dreams in the face of bleak reality combined in an impressive characterization.

Living between Two Worlds, directed by Robert Johnson, deals with the life of a black family in Los Angeles. A conflict between mother and son over differing life philosophies is one of the concerns of the plot. Though no award winner, it does highlight the conflicts that beset black families from within and without.

Jim Brown, the football player who decided to have a try at acting, was first seen in *Rio Conchos,* an incisive, well-made 1964 film. A Western with a Texas-Mexican setting in the post-Civil War period, it told the story of a squad of men, an ex-Confederate

officer, and a Mexican who conduct a search for a rifle shipment destined for Indians. Stuart Whitman and Richard Boone starred along with Brown who showed himself somewhat short on acting ability but long on charisma.

Brown rose rapidly during the sixties as the star of a series of action pictures such as *The Split* (1968) and *Riot* (1969), both about bloody prison breaks, and *100 Rifles,* a Western co-starring Raquel Welch. In all these films Brown exemplified the ideal physically and temperamentally healthy black. Though some black journalists deplored his consistent appearances in violent roles, they generally approved of his goal of providing young black boys with a strong hero to "identify like hell with."

The summer of 1964 marked the worst season of racial violence in twenty-one years. The films of 1965 that featured blacks were more concerned with drama and high adventure than with race relations. A number of these films featured blacks as accepted members of predominantly white groups.

Among a number of films to feature only one black man in a major role was *Cat Ballou,* in which Nat "King" Cole appeared as a traveling minstrel. This very funny film did not concern itself with race but busied itself with wild spoofing of every Western stereotype in film history.

In *Major Dundee,* released by Columbia and directed by the inventive Sam Peckinpah, a band of

Nat King Cole plays for Stubby Kaye in *Cat Ballou* (1965). Shelley Winters, center.

Roger Ewing and Rafer Johnson in *None But the Brave* (1965).

Union soldiers hunts Apache renegades in Mexico. Brock Peters, who already had a distinguished reputation for his fine performance in *To Kill a Mockingbird,* played a member of the U.S. Cavalry. Peckinpah, whose gift for pictorial composition and unique human delineation had caused him to rise in the Hollywood directorial hierarchy, brought a lot of action and drama into the film and drove home the point that blacks have performed as well as any other group in the armed services.

Rafer Johnson, another talented black actor, had a good role in an army picture that year, as an officer in Frank Sinatra's *None but the Brave,* a film involving military action on a small Pacific island during World War II.

Ossie Davis, who had made a name for himself on the New York stage, had a meaty role in *The Hill,* another 1965 army picture. The story was laid in a British detention camp in North Africa and concerned itself with the results of harsh disciplinary practices. Sidney Lumet directed. Harry Andrews, as head of the stockade, and Davis lent authentic human values to the film.

Cab Calloway, whose expert musicianship had enlivened many otherwise dull films, played a traveling cardsharp in *The Cincinnati Kid,* which dealt with the side streets of the gambling world and starred Steve McQueen and Edward G. Robinson as poker opponents. Calloway demonstrated a stunning

versatility in both musical and acting fields.

Another film in which a black actor's color had no integral bearing on the plot was *The Slender Thread.* In this film Anne Bancroft stars as a housewife who attempts to commit suicide, and Sidney Poitier portrays a college psychology student who by chance becomes involved in an effort to save her. The film featured good performances, naturalistic dialogue and good camera work. It was a trifle prosaic, but it held together well and was often both awesome and compelling.

Still in 1965, in *The Pawnbroker,* a low-budget film directed by Sidney Lumet, an effort was made to depict the misery of New York City's predominantly black Spanish Harlem. The picture dealt with the spiritual rebirth of Rod Steiger as a middle-aged Jewish survivor of a Nazi concentration camp. Through flashbacks to the man's past the film pointed out the similarities between the horrors of the concentration camp and the shockingly visualized ghetto—a prison in a supposedly free society.

The movie departed quite refreshingly from stereotypes by featuring black actor Brock Peters as a racketeer. This was Peters's second major role in a movie that year. As another change, the film's musical score was written by black composer Quincy Jones. Only very recently have blacks participated in the important behind-the-camera work of putting movies together.

A Patch of Blue, starring Sidney Poitier, was the only film of 1965 to direct its attention to the problems

(A) Sammy Davis, Jr., in *Man Called Adam* (1966). (B) Sidney Poitier and Ivan Dixon as brothers in *A Patch of Blue* (1965). (C) Poitier, Shelley Winters, and Elizabeth Hartman in the same film.

(A)

(B)

190

(C)

of race. It concerned a forlorn blind white girl, portrayed marvelously by Elizabeth Hartman, who is befriended by an intelligent and sensitive black man. She does not know or care about his color, but her mother, a whore, played rowdily by Shelley Winters, cares very much. Though sentimental, the film did underline the need for interracial compassion and cooperation, and its gentle romanticism contrasted favorably with some of the more violent fare making the rounds that year.

A Man Called Adam (1966) was produced by and starred Sammy Davis. Though it dealt pointedly with racial issues, the hero, a trouble-beset jazz trumpeter (Davis), had many personal problems as well. He was often shown in smokey clubs, sleazy bars, grim hotel rooms, wild jam sessions, and sinister back alleys.

Neurotic, self-pitying, and subtly self-destructive, the character as Davis played him was an authentic human being in the tradition of the realistic school. It demonstrated that Davis, in a role that gave him some characterizational leeway, could hold his own.

Louis Armstrong, who had redeemed many an otherwise unremarkable film like *Paris Blues* with his jazz, was present to contribute his usual fine work, this time as a bonus rather than a rescue operation.

The same year saw an effort to make up for years of scholarly neglect of black history, as Encyclopedia Britannica released a well-documented, if dramatically pedestrian, version of the life of Booker T. Washington.

Some producers may be confused by the subtleties of a changing movement not their own, but Otto Preminger is not among them. In his inimitable "Prussian general" style, he rushed in where angels feared to tread and came proudly out with *Hurry Sundown,* a total disaster of ugly stereotypes and anachronisms. The film featured Diahann Carroll, Robert Hooks, and Rex Ingram. A mishmash of foolish interracial romantic mischief and jumbled relationships, it stumbled out of bed just long enough to sketch out a plot about land developers versus resistant townspeople.

The blacks and their situations were portrayed in terms that would have been outrageous in 1936, let alone thirty years later. The romance, or rather sex, was handled in cheap theatrics.

In 1966 liberals of all colors moaned as Stokely Carmichael, the new leader of SNCC, denounced integration and proclaimed that what blacks needed was "black power." His ideas, however, were obviously in tune with many blacks' angry impatience with white paternalism, and the ideal of black power spread.

Guess Who's Coming to Dinner was a desperate attempt to ignore the changing times. Produced and directed by Stanley Kramer and written by William Rose, it cast Sidney Poitier in a shiny new affirmative stereotype. Poitier did his best, but his often-expressed aim of presenting to the public only positive images of the American Negro boomeranged badly.

Poitier's co-stars were the venerable team of Spencer Tracy (in his last film) and Katharine Hepburn and Miss Hepburn's niece Katharine Houghton. Hepburn played the mother of the girl, who is engaged to Poitier. Despite their liberalism, Hepburn and Tracy have difficulty swallowing the situation, even though Poitier is presented as witty, charming, brilliant and even, incredibly enough, a Noble Prize-winner. But the parents come around in the end, despite the warnings of their faithful black cook, who wants no truck with "uppity niggers."

Despite the abounding corn and the scriptwriter's overembroidery of the black potential son-in-law's character, the film was a box-office success.

Poitier next acted in To Sir, with Love (1967). Produced and directed by James Clavell and set in England, the story showcased Poitier in yet another of the affirmative incarnations to which the public had become accustomed. Here he played a compassionate and cultured engineer who, because of discrimination in his chosen field, is forced to spend a year teaching in a London slum school full of delinquent teenagers. Here he switched roles with Glenn Ford, who had played a similar part in a much rougher New York City environment in Blackboard Jungle. In the earlier film Poitier had been on the "side of the devils."

One black film that steered away from liberal mawkishness was In the Heat of the Night (1967), which co-starred Poitier and Rod Steiger in the role for which Steiger won an Oscar.

Directed with expertise by Norman Jewison, the film concerned a Northern detective, Poitier, assigned to help Steiger, bigoted police chief of a Southern town, solve a murder. This movie was a steamy drama of clashing personalities. The stern determination of

(Left) Sidney Poitier shakes hands with Spencer Tracy in *Guess Who's Coming to Dinner* (1967). Katharine Houghton is between them. (Above) Roy Glenn, Sr., and Beah Richards play Poitier's parents in the same film. Katharine Hepburn is opposite them.

Poitier shares a bench with Rod Steiger in the 1967 success *In The Heat of the Night.*

Poitier is juxtaposed against Steiger's redneck Southern malice, which eventually melts in the face of his reluctant admiration for the black man.

The film was admirable in its avoidance of lectures and clichés. There was no apologetic overwriting in Poitier's part this time, and instead of emphasizing condescending messages, the film's makers let their audience figure out the implications of the story for themselves. Not even the most radical militant could complain that Poitier's portrayal of the black detective lacked dignity.

Ossie Davis appeared the following year, 1968, in a Burt Lancaster vehicle, *The Scalphunters,* directed by Sidney Pollack. This Western farrago, shown from a comically inclined, well-meaning liberal viewpoint, featured Lancaster as a fur trapper and Davis as an erudite runaway slave, bound together by their mutual vulnerability to Indians and a band of white outlaws. The events, aided by exceptionally good dialogue, were played for laughs, aided by Telly Savalas as the chief scalphunter and Shelley Winters as a dizzy woman who

Quentin Dean, Poitier, James Patterson and Steiger in *Heat.*

Arnold Johnson and Alan Arbus in
Robert Downey's *Putney Swope* (1969).

(Left) Ossie Davis and Shelley Winters
in *The Scalphunters*. (1966).

traverses the plains in a frontier wagon equipped with such conveniences as a brass double bed. Lancaster and Davis eventually establish a grudging mutual admiration, and the film fades out with a tongue-in-cheek shot of the two riding off into the sunset together.

In 1968 Martin Luther King then Robert Kennedy were assassinated, followed by the debacle of the Chicago convention and the election of Richard Nixon. The optimistic feelings of the past began to seem hopelessly naïve.

Strangely enough, this turbulent year produced a startlingly refreshing output of films about black people. Some of these were outstanding for their sheer audacity. One such was veteran cameraman Haskell Wexler's first directorial effort, *Medium Cool,* an independently made film that made use of footage shot during the Chicago riots and contained some excellent and unprecedented material about blacks.

Though confusing in its efforts to touch on such varied topics as politics, violence, the responsibility of newsmen, and sexual values, the film presented an inside view of the black-militant scene that no conventional Hollywood director would have dared touch. In one scene the protagonist, a news cameraman, has to bargain with a group of black militants, who are menacingly seen through their victim's eyes until, in an exceptionally revealing moment just after he finally gets away, they slap hands and laugh at their own tough-man act.

This moment was very important because it let white viewers see the situation through black eyes. Wexler shot the scene with a group of nonactors who were basically portraying themselves. Every take required much suspicious probing of Wexler and a huddled black conference, until they were sure that they would come off on their own terms. Wexler has admitted that the process was extremely nerve-racking, but it was obviously worth it. This scene was a real first in its portrayal of militant blacks.

Wexler's courage was matched by the directors of two of the year's comedies.

In *Putney Swope,* also independently produced, director Robert Downey gleefully tore apart the myth of the black as a Goody Two Shoes. The black men in this movie were far too busy having a good time to be bothered with any Nobel prizes. *Putney* is the story of the accidentally inspired takeover of a large Madison Avenue advertising company by Mr. Swope, its sleepy-eyed black art director. Once he becomes chief, Swope turns the company upside-down and inside-out, firing whites, hiring blacks, renaming it Truth and Soul, Incorporated, and dedicating it to "telling it like it is." The resulting commercials are guaranteed to satisfy every television addict's wildest dreams.

Director Downey begins simply showing black men who actually enjoy living. But his daring soon grows as he mounts such scenes as the one in which Swope's black mistress starts really getting into the role of rich bitch, screaming at her white maid and slapping her around with shrewish abandon. Such displays of "white" behavior by successful blacks abound throughout the film.

Downey's audacity peaks when he finally undercuts even the most fashionable black stereotype, the smooth, silent, pistol-toting bodyguard. This character, who formerly seemed the coolest cat around next to Putney, when challenged to do anything more than pose photogenically, is suddenly shown as a blundering fool who has to have his gun tied to him with string.

It took daring for a white director to poke fun at this symbol of a new, tough, black self-image. In doing so, Downey dared to treat blacks as full-fledged human beings. It is hardly surprising that this movie emerged from the New York "underground" rather than from the cautious studios of Hollywood. It made a lot of money—a hopeful sign that a growing audience was fed up with being protected from satire about sensitive issues.

During the sixties the film industry finally made some effort to free itself from the caution of the fifties, attempting to chronicle the changes that gripped the nation. Unfortunately, for most of its efforts were weak, stumbling a few paces behind events. Yet progress was being made. For the first time in film history, there were serious attempts to portray the black experience. The number of Oscar nominations and awards made to films related to black subjects make it obvious that the industry itself was taking these attempts seriously.

Hollywood's good intentions opened up many job opportunities to black actors and eventually to blacks interested in working behind the camera. And though many attempts to portray black life met with mawkish failure, lessons were learned.

The last year of the decade showed the black cinema's coming of age. At last, the drama and humor of black life could stand by themselves.

The efforts of the independent filmmaking movement had formed a cosmopolitan, aware audience large enough to support films catering to its tastes. In an atmosphere of unprecedented cynicism, an "anything goes" atmosphere arose among filmmakers, resulting in films more daring and outspoken than any before them. In 1969, it looked as if the seventies would be a truly exciting era for black movies.

A portfolio of scenes from the 1960's

Hugh Hurd (left) and Lelia Goldoni in
Cassavettes' *Shadows* (1961).

Odetta and Lee Remick in the 1961 version of Faulkner's
Sanctuary.

(Left) James Whitmore and Roscoe Lee
Brown in *Black Like Me* (1964).

Claudia Cardinale is held by Woody Strode as Lee Marvin grimaces in *The Professionals* (1966).

Abbey Lincoln and Ivan Dixon in *Nothing But a Man* (1964).

Shirley Knight and Al Freeman, Jr., in *Dutchman* (1967).

Beah Richards and Robert Hooks in *Hurry Sundown*, an Otto Preminger failure in 1966.

Sidney Poitier and Richard Widmark in *The Bedford Incident* (1965)

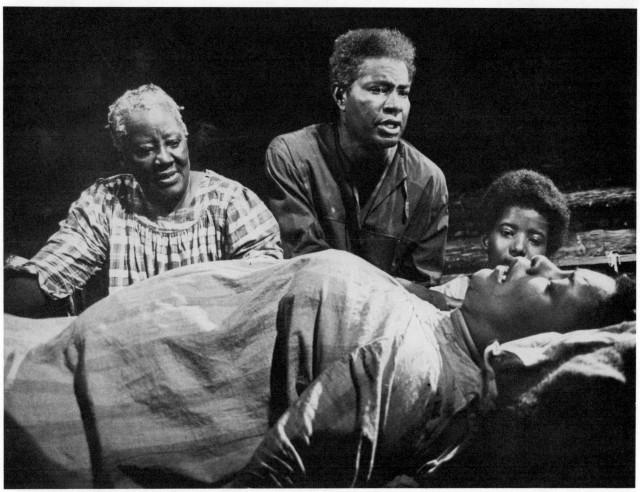

Eva Jessye, Ossie Davis and Adline King in *Slaves* (1969).

Jim Brown and Raquel Welch in *100 Rifles* (1968).

Ruby Dee, Godfrey Cambridge, Ossie Davis and Alan Alda in the screen version of *Purlie Victorious* (1963).

Sidney Poitier, Bill Travers and James Garner in *Duel at Diablo* (1966).

Rupert Crosse and Steve McQueen in *The Reivers* (1969).

Sidney Poitier and Al Freeman, Jr., face
Joanna Shimkus in *The Lost Man* (1969).

Sidney Poitier over a prostrate Bernie
Hamilton in the same film.

Ruby Dee and Brock Peters in *The Incident* (1967).

Peter Brocco kisses Ruby Dee's toe in a fantasy scene from *The Balcony* (1963).

Chapter 7
The Seventies

(A)

It is impossible to predict where black Hollywood will go in the seventies. More and more filmmakers are financing small, independent efforts. The growing emphasis on local organization and community control has its influence at the artistic level, and many exciting things are happening in small but important experimental black theater groups, as well as in films made independently by blacks. However, what such embryo movements hold for the future is uncertain, depending largely on finding a way to circumvent the power of the major distribution channels.

Of course, the commercial film structure is as powerful as ever. Its stranglehold on distribution is being challenged, but the major studios still have the capacity to influence millions of people, even if audiences are becoming more sophisticated.

The most important new development is the emergence of truly black films, which are not merely vehicles for black actors but are directed by blacks and destined for a black audience whose self-confidence has increased enormously.

Following Gordon Parks' landmark *The Learning Tree* by less than a year came *Cotton Comes to Harlem*, 1970's first black film with a black director. It starred Godfrey Cambridge, directed by Ossie Davis. Davis, who had frequently put his career on the line by speaking up for black causes, knew he'd be stepping on a number of toes in making a *comedy* about Harlem. Even while making the film he encountered hostility from some Harlem residents who thought he should be doing something more militant. Some young black members of the movie's Ford Foundation-financed apprenticeship program (founded to help blacks increase their ranks behind the camera) were uncooperative because they, too, felt that this was no time to make comedies about the ghetto.

Davis countered these criticisms with the statement that "In Harlem you have to have a sense of humor. The only people who could deal with rats and filth are those with a sense of humor."

Luckily, Davis stuck to his guns and, for the first time on the screen, produced a very funny, solidly black film. The movie was full of black stereotypes no white director would have dared to include, but they delighted the majority of the black audience that flocked to see it. The film was a great financial success and opened up the market for black movies made by blacks.

Scenes from
Cotton
Comes To Harlem
(1970)

(A) Raymond St. Jacques and Godfrey Cambridge contemplate a smashed windshield. (B) St. Jacques and Cambridge.

Redd Foxx and J. D. Cannon in *Cotton Comes to Harlem*.

Mabel Robinson.

Cambridge restrains St. Jacques., Judy Pace.

In many films of the new black Hollywood, there is much cynicism. Gone are socially relevant movies of the sixties, which often treated the race issue with insulting oversensitivity. Those films were usually directed by whites and appealed to white liberal audiences who shared directors' aspirations.

Now we have the emergence of black directors and black stars with an entirely different approach. Most of the new commercial black movies are similar in some ways to those of Hollywood in the thirties, with the emphasis overwhelmingly on entertainment.

The screen images of black life reflect the new confidence of black people. They also reflect the political movement towards separatism, because today's black commercial films are meant for black audiences, no longer dependent on a white audience's approval to be financially successful. Today's black-directed, almost all-black films no longer depict blacks' striving for recognition by white society; they depict blacks' deep desire for self-affirmation.

The unimpeachable behavior of Poitier and Belafonte, which seemed to plead for tolerance and understanding, did not really reflect the lives of black people. Nor, of course, do the new, tough, sexually potent and very-much-in-control images of such rising stars as Jim Brown and Richard Roundtree. Most of the films in which these actors appear are escapist fantasies in which violence is the new romanticism.

What emerges, in fact, is an altogether new set of black stereotypes. Perhaps derived from the movement toward black power, the cool, efficient black hero seems to have more in common with James Bond than with the political ideals of any black movement. Some of these movies pay lip service to black separatism, Afro-American culture, and local control, but the image seems to betray a stake in white America, with a new breed of spies, secret-service agents, supercriminals, and superhip cops. The black audience can identify with these heroes simply because they have changed color and speak a slightly different kind of English—but even the jargon influences whites just as much as it reflects black life.

However, although the stars of the black movies often seem two-dimensional, and the plots seem to be nothing but vehicles for violence, these films are important from the point of view of group identification. Also, directors are beginning to use movies to show areas of black history that have only recently been seriously researched. The real expression of black consciousness is beginning to find its way onto the screen.

Although both black and white critics have expressed anxiety over the trend toward violence, the violence of such films as *Shaft* (1971), *The Slams* (1973), *Slaughter's Big Rip-off* (1973), *Coffy* (1973), *Gordon's War* (1973), and *Trouble Man* (1973), while excessive, seem to serve as a catharsis. It has been suggested that in these films, the pent-up frustrations of the black audience find an outlet and that "black exploitation" films use violence in a highly ritualized way. It is certainly true that in watching Jim Brown or Richard Roundtree a black audience is able to identify with the emotions of the protagonist in a way the white public could not.

Jim Brown, though not a great actor, is the personification of the local boy who made good by being bad. Ex football player Brown is the tough ghetto stud who acts out the fantasies of frustrated high school kids as he slams his fist in the face of the society that made him so violent—and always wins. In *The Slams* he is a convict determined to keep his hands on the fortune he has stolen. In *Slaughter's Big Rip-off*, he fights the syndicate that tried to get rid of him.

One of the first superviolent films was *Shaft*, which introduced Richard Roundtree, one of the most demanded black stars. Directed by Gordon Parks, the film features Roundtree, the cool black stud, as a private eye in the Bogart tradition. Living elegantly in a Greenwich Village duplex and dressed in style, Shaft clashes brutally with everyone including the police, the Mafia, and black militants. He is, of course, utterly fearless and unbeatable.

Interestingly, black audiences take Roundtree's black detective for granted. There is no departure here —only Shaft's accessories are black; he represents the larger white Hollywood culture of Bogart, Wayne, and Connery.

Unlike Brown, to whom toughness is all, Roundtree is a talented performer whose characterizations are as well rounded as the scripts allow. The critics referred to *Shaft* as "a fast-moving pleasure," "a fine Saturday-night movie," and "an enjoyable, suspenseful who's-doing-it."

Roundtree displayed considerable *élan* in his performance and received glowing notices such as "makes an authentic star debut" and "reason enough to see the movie."

Some critics, however, were disturbed by the film's violence, cynical approach to serious racial and sociological situations, which they saw as socially deleterious. The stereotyped supercop is no more admirable now, say these critics, than was the clownish foolery of Stepin Fetchit in the twenties. The difference is that whereas Stepin Fetchit's roles were intended to

A 1971 hit, *Shaft*, starred Richard Roundtree (right) with Sherri Brewer and Christopher St. John.

Stella Stevens and Jim Brown in *Slaughter* (1972).

(B)

(Left above) Two scenes from *Shaft in Africa* (1973). (A) Roundtree and Vonetta McGee. (B) Roundtree struggles with Spiro Focas.

211

(A)

Ron O'Neal (right) with Carl Lee.

With Sheila Frazier.

Ron O'Neal.

entertain white audiences, the suave Mr. Roundtree
fulfills the fantasies of largely black audiences.

Shaft was a frankly commercial film, as was its
successor Shaft's Big Score, made in 1972, and all its
imitators, from Super Fly on. Super Fly, made in 1972,
also by Gordon Parks, and independently financed by a
group of black businessmen, featured Ron O'Neal as a
cocaine dealer, who outwits the system and everyone
else. Needless to say, Super Fly was heavily criticized
for making the pusher into a cult folk-hero; yet in some
respects Super Fly was a little nearer to reality than
some of the others.

(A)

(B)

(A) Lola Falana and Anthony Zerbe.
(B) Fayard Nicholas, Roscoe Lee Brown,
Yaphet Kotto. (C) Nicholas and Lauren
Jones.

Scenes from
Sweet Sweetback's
Baadasss Song
(1971)

Another point of criticism is that the sexuality of films of this genre is reminiscent of the sensuous black-brute image that so horrified the audiences at Griffith's films. The image of the black man as spectacularly potent stud, firmly fixed in both black and white imaginations, had not been allowed on the screen since the 1920s. It made its reappearance in Melvin Van Peebles' *Sweet Sweetback's Baadasssss Song* (1971), in which Van Peebles starred as the pimp hero. This was another romanticization-of-violence film, exciting, flamboyant, and controversial. It was condemned for its gratuitous sexuality, which seemed to depict all black women as whores in a black man's world.

The role of black women in films, always previously confined to servant roles, with only white-looking women being allowed to be sexually alluring (and sinful), did not reflect their status in the black community, in which women have always been far more important and far stronger than their white sisters. It is curious, then, that in most of the new black films, women were treated as mere sex objects, part of the superficial fantasy lives of the heroes. Two 1973 films, *Coffy* and *Cleopatra Jones,* used women as the hero figures. In *Coffy,* a particularly violent movie, the main character (Pam Grier) is a nurse who seeks revenge on a dope pusher. The film concentrates on violence, and the main character's sex is merely a

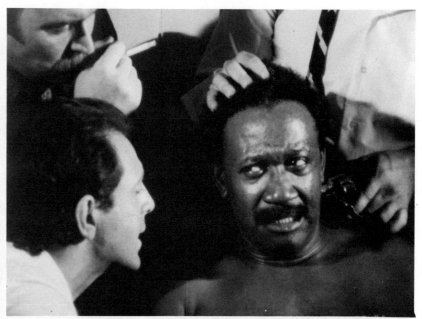

Simon Chuckster.

Melvin Van Peebles.

Melvin Van Peebles.

Tamara Dobson.

Miss Dobson in a karate pose.

gimmick. *Cleopatra Jones,* however, was a far superior movie. Starring Tamara Dobson as a secret agent, it seemed to owe something to the popular *Avengers* TV series, made in England, which featured a woman karate expert who was also a special agent. Miss Dobson uses spectacular tactics to defeat her enemies, who are headed by a white female drug pusher (Shelley Winters), and she is spectacular in her beauty. If black movies have hardly begun to elevate women to real character roles, at least the white-dominated ideas of beauty are gone. At last, very dark-skinned, African-looking women appear on the screen to prove that the slogan "black is beautiful" has become an integral part of black culture.

Apart from these films, which appear to represent a new genre, several films since 1970 have continued the more positive values of the sixties. These films, especially the ones with Sidney Poitier, James Earl Jones, or Brock Peters, seem curiously distant from the new black-directed films. Still struggling with interracial issues, these stars are often accused of being Uncle Tom characters, concerned with projecting a socially redeeming character. The message of such movies is often highly didactic and not always to their advantage. This feeling is well described by Brock Peters, who said of Poitier,

Miss Dobson's battle with Shelley Winters.

There are many ways of projecting a character, and I think the mold that Poitier perhaps fits best is, of course, what we describe as the leading man, the chief protagonist of the story. There is, in my view, a strict limitation of a kind imposed on an actor who plays starring parts and/or leading roles. It is essential that he evoke response, empathy, sympathy from his audience. So he has to be very careful about the extremes of emotion he projects. They cannot be too far left or right; they must be emotions most people can deal with without greatly disturbing themselves.

On the other hand, a character actor can strike right at the truth of the thing and create, as pertinently and graphically as possible, the emotions of the moment in a given situation. He doesn't find it necessary to temper his characterizations with diplomacy.

An example of what Peters meant is seen in *They Call Me Mister Tibbs,* in which Poitier portrays his detective as a mysterious, almost Christ-like figure as he solves the murder of a white friend. The characterization seems forced, not up to the standard of his earlier films. He appears to be concerned primarily with presenting middle-class black family life in its very best light, concentrating on the detective's relationship with his small son in some tender scenes.

Another Poitier film, *For Love of Ivy* (1968), also failed to reach the high standards of his earlier output. As with *Mister Tibbs,* the idea of the film was conceived by Poitier and written in collaboration with Robert Alan Aurthur. A light comedy in which Abbey Lincoln starred opposite Poitier, it describes the romance of a trucking entrepreneur who likes to gamble. Miss Lincoln is a maid in a liberal white household in Long Island. The film is highly moralistic, and Poitier is fervently committed to depicting, with some integrity, a picture of "ordinary" black life.

Buck and the Preacher (1972) indicated that Poitier might be advancing both as an actor and as a director into subjects more relevant to the seventies. *Buck and the Preacher* is a historical film about an ex Union-cavalry officer (Poitier) leading a group of former slaves to new homes in the West. The Preacher is played by Harry Belafonte, an old friend on screen and off. The serious film tries to tackle the historical subject truthfully and to deal with the reasons for oppression. It ends on a triumphant note. It was successful at the box office, proving popular with both black and white audiences.

Poitier's importance as a black actor and as an ambassador for his race is unquestionable. Among actors, Poitier, more than any other person, helped

(Above) Paul Udell holds the mike for Juano Hernandez and Sidney Poitier in *They Call Me Mr. Tibbs* (1970).

(Right) Poitier and Beau Bridges in *For the Love of Ivy* (1968).

(A)

establish better relations between blacks and whites, whether or not black radicals admit the worth of this. He also considerably opened up the film medium to black performers. To do this, he had to be acceptable to white audiences and, more importantly, to white producers. If his role now seems a little hackneyed, this should not take away from his very real achievement.

In a 1968 article on Poitier in *Screen Parade,* Lawrence J. Quirk summed up the attitude not only of Poitier, but of the group of actors who became prominent in the sixties and who seem in the seventies to be searching for a new means of expressing their roles.

Sidney Poitier is no sentimentalist. He has no patience with vague panaceas for the world's heartbreaking problems. He considers concepts like brotherly love too vague to take hold in reality or to be spelled out in action.

Rather he plumps for what is most deeply human in us all . . . the consummate human essence, the mystic instinct that makes us all one. And he asks, in his person and in his performances, that we act upon that essence and that instinct, and work together to make strengthful realistic love, spelled out in badly needed social, economic, and institutional reforms, our aim and our consuming goal.

Love in action and love in dreams are two different things, he implies. To deal with the world as one finds it, to make the necessary compromises . . . with the overall goal of greater human solidarity, among all races and creeds, a hand-in-hand struggle for human betterment, takes a realistic, not a sentimental, approach.

(B)

(A) Harry Belafonte, Ruby Dee and
Sidney Poitier. (B) The film's three stars.
(C) Belafonte.

(C)

Another film on a historical subject centered, like the later *Buck and the Preacher,* on slavery. *Slaves* (1969) found Ossie Davis in what some critics dubbed a 1970-style Uncle Tom role. Stephen Boyd plays a plantation owner who has gone to the dogs, and Dionne Warwick plays his bitter black mistress bent on revenge and corruption. The brutality of the plantation situation is portrayed in lurid terms; it is very different from that sunny place where the darkies used to toil and sing so contentedly just a few decades ago.

Ossie Davis leads the slave rebellion and attempts to link contemporary black militancy with the

Clarence Muse.

Roscoe Lee Brown and Clarence Muse in *The World's Greatest Athlete* (1972).

antebellum past. The most interesting concept in the film is that the hated master has decorated his house with African art, and he comments on the African heritage throughout. However the sociological value of the film is questionable, for with its emphasis on violence and sex, it is plainly concerned primarily with entertainment.

Ossie Davis directed the controversial *Cotton Comes to Harlem,* of which *The New York Times'* critic wrote,

> I was also reminded of Oscar Micheaux, who in the 1920s and 1930s made black films for black theaters modeled on white movie stereotypes. Aside from its honest black idioms and actors, *Cotton Comes to Harlem* is a conventional white movie which employs some terrible white stereotypes of black life.

To other critics, *Cotton Comes to Harlem* was a highly enjoyable and ironical comment on the stereotypes blacks had imposed on themselves by accepting white images and turning them into something else.

Five on the Black Hand Side (1973) modernized the stereotypes. Directed by Oscar Williams, this film was hailed as a truthful comedy about black life. It contained a great deal of *élan* but merely added a few additional black stereotypes.

In this film a tyrannical father, the head of a Harlem household, keeps his wife in unbelievable subjugation. His daughter is about to be married in an African ceremony, and one of his two sons works for the community but keeps a white girlfriend, about whom only allusions are made. This son's integrationist tendencies are condemned by his militant younger brother, a caricature of the "new black man." Unfortunately, since this film is a comedy, the brothers' political aspirations are made to seem comical, as is women's liberation when the downtrodden wife rebels.

The family is reunited in the daughter's African wedding ceremony, with everyone in costume, as the theme of Afro-American unity emerges.

The funniest scenes of the film take place in the father's barbershop, where a parade of pimps, shoeshine boys, militants, and criminals make an ironic commentary on the state of the black film, with its mélange of commercialized values. No whites appear in this film.

Two 1970 films alluded to the problems of interracial marriage. Totally different from each other in approach and treatment, both *The Landlord* and *The*

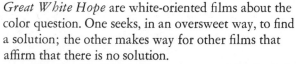
Glynn Turman and D'Urville Martin in *Five on the Black Hand Side* (1973).

Carl Mikal Franklin and Bonnie Banfield.

Great White Hope are white-oriented films about the color question. One seeks, in an oversweet way, to find a solution; the other makes way for other films that affirm that there is no solution.

The Landlord is in many ways a truthful depiction of the white liberal attitudes of the sixties. Beau Bridges plays a young man from a rich family with a romantic desire to live among and give aid to the black neighbors in the Brooklyn slum where he has bought a house. His strong feelings about racial equality are not shared by his new neighbors. The blacks are hostile, he gets a black woman pregnant, he nearly gets killed, and he finally moves out.

The film gets involved with too many side issues, which confuse the point it is trying to make. At the end, Bridges adopts his son by the black woman,

Clarice Taylor and Virginia Capers (right).

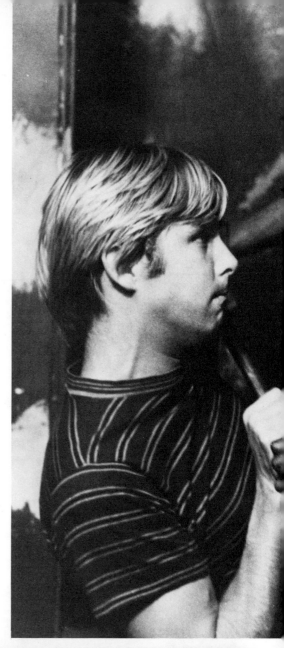

Pearl Bailey and Lee Grant in *The Landlord*.

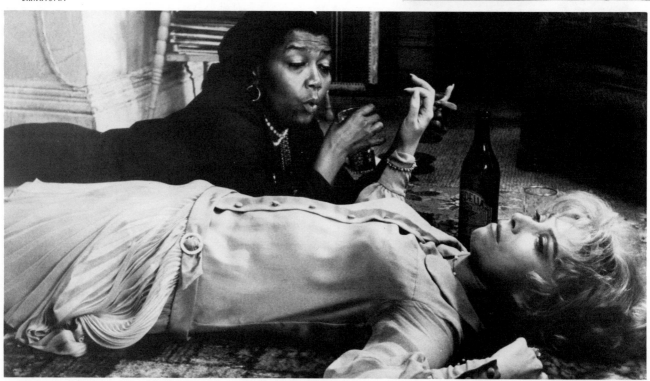

Beau Bridges and Lou Gossett in *The Landlord* (1970).

because her alliance with a black man makes it impossible for her to keep the child. Presumably sadder but wiser, the young idealist rides away with the child in his car.

Black journalists considered this film psychologically unsound, but some praised the honesty of its attempt at better racial understanding.

The Great White Hope attempts to present an in-depth study of the effects of racism on a human being—in this case, Jack Jefferson (James Earl Jones), the first black to become heavyweight boxing champion of the world. The film was based on the Broadway play of the same name and both were based on the actual life story of Jack Johnson, the first black to win the title, in 1908. This achievement is so infuriating to the white-supremacist powers of the boxing world that they are determined to ruin him.

Jefferson is not only victorious in the ring, but he also has a white mistress (Jane Alexander), whom he flaunts in public. His enemies have him arrested and convicted on trumped-up charges. Forced to flee the country, he wanders from place to place until he finally has no other recourse but to return to the United States and his final tragic defeat.

The Great White Hope is a triumph for the acting of James Earl Jones, but it received mixed reviews. It brutally reveals the white man's need to maintain a sense of racial superiority at all costs, and it treats with compassion the previously taboo subject of interracial love.

Hollywood obviously felt that in 1970 the theme of interracial hatred had become respectable, especially if it were placed safely in the past.

Yet in another 1970 film, *The Liberation of L. B.*

(A) Jane Alexander and James Earl Jones.
(B) Jack Johnson, here named Jack
Jefferson, throws a heavy punch at Larry
Pennell as the former champion in an
exciting ring scene.

Scenes from
The Great White Hope
(1970)

(B)

(A)

Jones, the implicit idea is that blacks and whites cannot co-exist. A black liberal (Roscoe Lee Browne) is liberated when he divorces his wife, who has been having an affair with a white man. Thus Browne sets in motion his own black consciousness. The liberation is completed by a thorough and violent revenge by a young radical (Yaphet Kotto), who, in killing a white farmer by pushing him into his own baler, seems to prepare the way for revolution.

This film was both violent and commercially oriented. It showed, as Vincent Canby said in his review in *The New York Times,*

When William Wyler . . . makes such a vivid, melodramatic rationale for the collapse of race relations that the movie comes close to celebrating it, you had better believe that something is happening in this land. Political polarization has at last become the kind of reality in which Hollywood can invest several million dollars as a source for popular entertainment.

In 1973, Ivan Dixon directed *The Spook Who Sat by the Door.* Superficially, this film has points in common with other black-genre movies, with its extreme use of violence, its superstud sexuality, its indigenous streetcorner pusher, and its premise of black superiority. However, in *Spook* the violence is never gratuitous and is always subdued, the streetcorner pusher is a mean and pitiful victim of an unjust society and the sexuality is handled with almost prudish delicacy.

In *The Spook Who Sat by the Door,* Lawrence Cook trains with the CIA, as the agency's only black. Posing as a meek, self-effacing but efficient officer, he becomes the "director's nigger" and after five years becomes a social worker in Chicago. Here he sets about training a street gang in the use of CIA-inspired guerrilla warfare in preparation for the bloodbath that will erupt with the next riot. When this occurs, crack troops of a grass-roots black army will be ready to take over the means to their new statehood.

The Spook Who Sat by the Door is by no means a great film. The acting is wooden at times, some of the characterizations, especially of white people, are two dimensional, and some of the situations lack credibility. Yet the film seems totally sincere in its premise that revolution is the only answer for blacks.

The Spook Who Sat by the Door is reminiscent of *State of Siege,* the Costa-Gavras film about the Tupamaros guerrillas, both in the relentless unfolding of events and in its clear statement of its political purpose. Yet *Spook* is not a political film striving to inform an educated public. It is a commercial movie. Does the production of such a film indicate that black separatism has become acceptable in the same way that interracial friendship became respectable in the fifties? In any event, *The Spook Who Sat by the Door* steps out of fantasy into reality and indicates that perhaps in the future black films will be truly separate from white films.

Sounder (1972) is a unique and original film. It did not follow the tasteless assembly-line black films that exploited the black film market during the previous four years. Instead, it dealt honestly and sensitively with the day-to-day struggle for survival of a black family living in a small rural area of the South during the Depression. The plot was simple and uncomplicated, and the acting was exceptional, especially that of Cicely Tyson, who was nominated for the Academy Award for best actress.

Sounder concentrated on character development rather than on a fast-paced story. In trying to make ends meet and keep her family fed, clothed, and schooled after her husband is jailed for stealing a ham, Cicely Tyson presented a *tour de force.*

The film vividly followed Miss Tyson through each hot, sweaty day of work and frustration and each night of loneliness. Throughout, she tries to show her twelve-year-old son the importance of making it out of the hell that he has been forced to live in. The boy's struggle and his conflict about leaving home are among the film's important points.

In the end, after his father has been released from prison, he does leave home to go to school and improve his chances of getting out of the cycle of poverty.

Black Hollywood has had a checkered, uphill history that, until this decade, did not allow a true expression of black people. From the time that blackfaced white actors began appearing in the silent movies until the mid-fifties, when Sidney Poitier appeared, the roles portrayed by blacks were entirely reflective of white attitudes toward blacks. Then, just as the oppressive stereotypes figures of idiot servant, savage brute, big black mammy, watermelon eater, hymn singer, and natural-rhythm man seemed to be gone forever, and it seemed as if real, live black human beings were finally acceptable, a new set of black stereotypes emerged.

These new stereotypes express the images black screenwriters, producers, and directors have of their race. They will be replaced in time by something else. Hollywood does not innovate; it reflects and reinforces already accepted images. Perhaps black Hollywood's safe attitudes are changing, but perhaps it is society that is changing and filmmakers are becoming more sensitive to the historical process.

Paul Winfield and Kevin Hooks.

(A)

(B)

(C)

(A) The dog, Sounder, is restrained as the sheriff arrests Paul Winfield. (B) Father embraces his son through the prison bars. (C) The reunion. (D) Winfield, Yvonne Jarrell, Eric Hooks and Taj Mahal make their way home following an afternoon baseball game. (E) Cicely Tyson, who received an Academy Award nomination for her performance, with Kevin Hooks as her son.

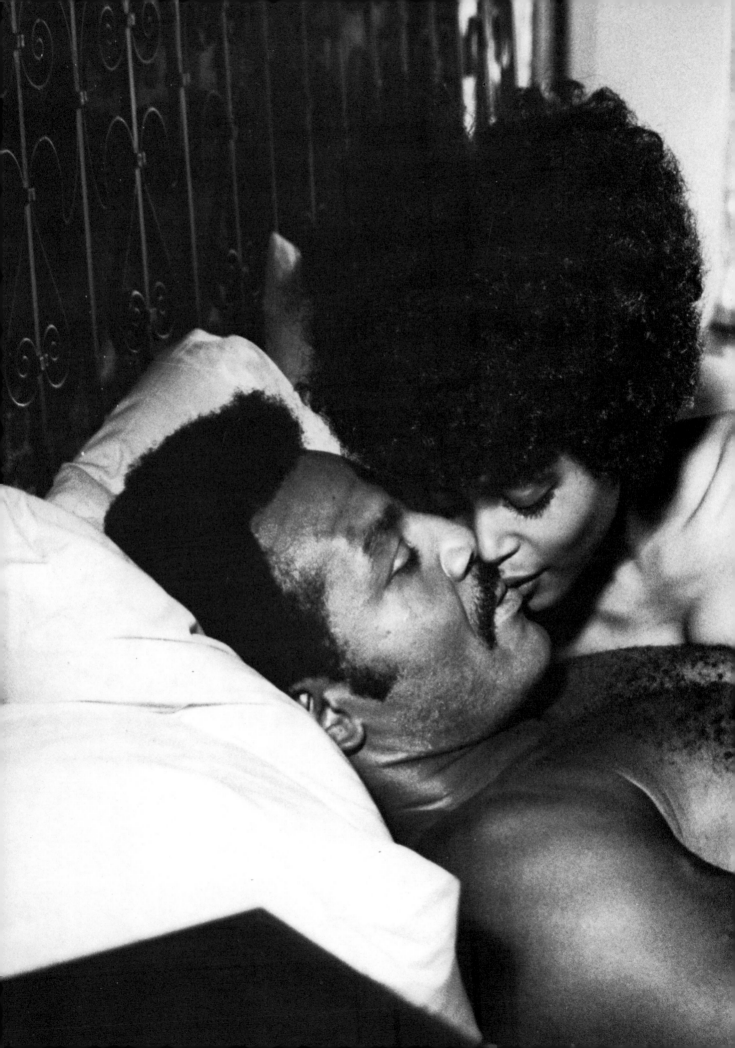

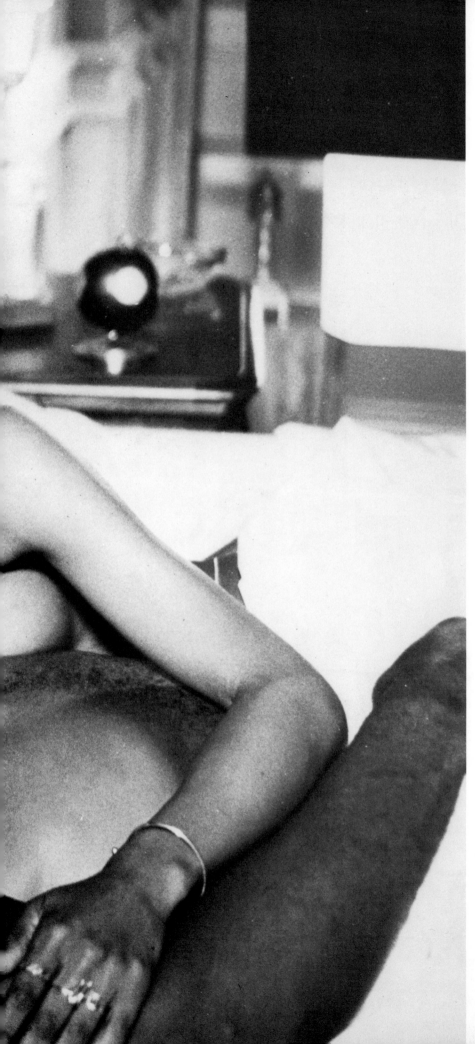

Jim Brown and Brenda Sykes in *Black Gunn* (1972).

Scenes from
Watermelon Man
(1970)

James Garner and Lou Gosset in *The Skin Game* (1971).

Calvin Lockhart and Paul Stevens in *Melinda* (1972).

(A) Godfrey Cambridge under Melvin Van Peebles' direction. (B) Godfrey Cambridge as a white man. (C) Estelle Parsons and their children face the now-black husband and father. (D) Mantan Moreland and Cambridge.

Marlene Warfield, Yaphet Kotto and Anthony Quinn in *Across 110th Street* (1972).

(A) Dirk Benedict and Diana Sands in *Georgia, Georgia* (1972). (B) Godfrey Cambridge in *Come Back, Charleston Blue* (1972). (C) Robert Hooks, reflected in mirrors, wins a shoot-out with Ralph Waite in *Trouble Man* (1972). (D) Hooks and Paula Kelly in the same film.

(B)

(A)

(D)

(C)

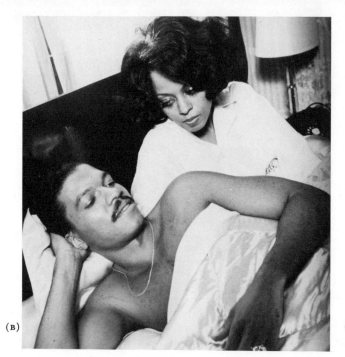

(A)

(B)

(C)

(D)

(A) Diana Ross as Billie Holiday.
(B) With Billy Dee Williams. (C) A tense
moment with Williams. (D) With Richard
Pryor.

(A)

(B)

Scenes from
Heavy Traffic
(1973)

(c)

(A) The Hookers. (B) Beverly Hope
Atkinson and Joseph Kaufman.
(C) Animation.

(A)

(B)

Scenes from
Uptown Saturday Night
(1974)

(c)

(A) Johnny Sekka, Harry Belafonte, Sidney
Poitier and Bill Cosby. (B) Bill Cosby and
Fayard Nicholas. (C) Poitier, Belafonte,
Cosby.

(A)

(B)

(A) Fred Williamson and Tricia O'Neil in *The Legend of Nigger Charlie* (1972). (B) Peter Boyle and Fred Williamson (Right) in *Crazy Joe* (1973). (C) Jon Voight in *Conrack* (1974). (D) Diahann Carroll and James Earl Jones in *Claudine* (1974).

(D)

(A)

(c)

(D)

(A) Moms Mabley and Slappy White in
Amazing Grace (1974). (B) Butterfly
McQueen. (c) Madeleine Kahn and Cleavon
Little in *Blazing Saddles* (1974).
(D) Ciaran Madden, Peter Cushing, and
Calvin Lockheart in *The Beast Must Die*
(1974).

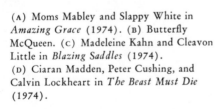

B)

(Left) Tamara Dobson in *Cleopatra Jones Meets the Dragon Princess* (1975).